6/23/12

THE GLORIES OF

CZESTOCHOWA AND JASNA GORA

MIRACLES ATTRIBUTED TO OUR LADY'S INTERCESSION

Dear Fr. Maximilian,

May our Lady of Czestochowa always guide you, protect you and keep you in her heart.

God bless you

Dorota Hejno

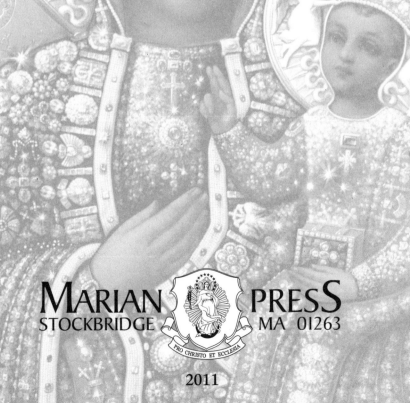

THE GLORIES OF
CZESTOCHOWA AND JASNA GORA
MIRACLES ATTRIBUTED TO OUR LADY'S INTERCESSION

MARIAN PRESS
STOCKBRIDGE · MA 01263

PRO CHRISTO ET ECCLESIA

2011

Available from:
Marian Helpers Center
Stockbridge, MA 01263

Prayers: 1-800-804-382
Orders: 1-800-462-7426
Website: www.marian.org

First published in 1955 for Our Lady of Czestochowa Foundation, Diocese of Worcester, Massachusetts.

Imprimatur: Most Rev. John J. Wright, D.D.
Bishop of Worcester
March 25, 1955
Feast of the Annunciation

Translated from the original Polish, which was approved and then published by ecclesiastical authorities in Poland.

Library of Congress Catalog Number
2004104412

ISBN
978-1-932773-97-2

Front Cover: The miraculous image of Our Lady of Czestochowa at Jasna Gora in Poland. Reproduction copyright © 2004 Marian Fathers of the Immaculate Conception of the B.V.M.

Printed in the United States of America by Marian Press

TABLE OF CONTENTS

FOREWORD

All Christians are called to live a life of holiness by faithfully following our Lord Jesus Christ, the Savior of the world. They are called to know, love, and serve the Lord more and more each day and to be imbued with His Spirit. The goal is for Christ to be proclaimed to all the nations and all peoples, so everyone can experience His healing and transforming gift of love and mercy.

In imitating the life of Christ and participating in the mystery of His redemption, it is fruitful to keep before our eyes Mary, the humble handmaid of the Lord. In the Church, she is a model of perfect openness to the Father's will, of obedience to the inspiration of the Holy Spirit, and of profound union with Jesus, her Divine Son.

As the Immaculate Virgin and Our Blessed Mother, she shows us the way to a relationship with God, who is Love and Mercy Itself, and assists us in our daily struggles with her powerful protection. She is a special sign, strength, and joy of the Christian vocation. She never ceases to call us to place our trust in the unlimited fruitfulness of the work of her Son's redemption, to avoid all sin, to hold in the highest esteem purity of heart, and to live a life fully immersed in divine grace and love in order to be holy and immaculate.

May all Christians go through the Immaculate Mother of God to her Son, Jesus. As in the miraculous accounts recorded in *The Glories of Czestochowa and Jasna Gora*, may they turn to her with the greatest confidence in all their needs, and receive abundant blessings from the infinite fountain of grace and mercy pouring forth through her from her Divine Son. *Ave Maria!*

— The Marian Fathers of the Immaculate Conception

PREFACE

The Mother of Our Saviour, Jesus Christ, is known under diverse titles throughout many lands. For the Polish people, wherever they may be found, she is best known and most beloved under the title of Our Lady of Czestochowa, whose miraculous image has been preserved for centuries at Jasna Gora in Czestochowa, Poland.

Our Lady of Czestochowa is for the Poles what Our Lady of Lourdes is for the French, and Our Lady of Fatima is for the Portuguese. The history, traditions and miracles of Czestochowa are the heritage of the Polish people. Unlike the shrines at Lourdes and Fatima, the shrine at Czestochowa has not acquired world-wide renown and international popularity, so that many who are not familiar with the Polish language know very little of the wonders associated with Czestochowa.

Miracles there appear to have been numerous. Indeed, they are well known to the people of Poland. For that reason, the shrine at Czestochowa has enjoyed a steady stream of pilgrims from all parts of Poland as well as from the surrounding countries where the fame of Czestochowa has spread.

Those whose good fortune has brought them in contact with the Miraculous Image or copies thereof, whether in their travels or by visits to local churches where Our Lady of Czestochowa is enshrined, have become familiar with the dark-toned image with two pronounced scars on the cheek. Particularly noteworthy is a copy of the Miraculous Image placed in a private chapel of the Vatican by Pope Pius XI, who, after serving as Apostolic Nuncio to Poland, brought the picture to Rome as a memento of his stay in Poland. The Pope dedicated the chapel in honor of Our Lady of Czestochowa as a manifestation of his love for her and his paternal concern for the people of Poland.

Most of the parish churches serving the Polish people in our diocese have beautiful shrines dedicated to Our Lady of Czestochowa. A shrine is also found in St. Paul's Cathedral in Worcester; many who had never seen a picture of Our Lady of Czestochowa have come to know her because of this.

Although many have become acquainted with the Miraculous Image of Our Lady of Czestochowa, few are acquainted with the history of its numerous miracles. These miracles have often provided themes in Polish literature, but little has been available in the English language concerning them. In order to give us all an opportunity to become acquainted with the history of the miracles of Czestochowa, the Polish speaking clergy of the Diocese of Worcester have prepared this publication. The book is a labor of love on their part and recounts many of the miracles performed through the intercession of Our Lady of Czestochowa. The original accounts of these are preserved in the archives of the Pauline Fathers at Jasna Gora, to whose care the Miraculous Image has been entrusted throughout the centuries.

The purpose of the **Glories of Czestochowa and Jasna Gora** is to spread the fame of our Lady of Czestochowa far and wide and thus add to the motives for love of the Blessed Mother which characterize our people. May she bless the priests who have been so eager to proclaim her praises!

— Bishop of Worcester

History of the Miraculous Portrait of Our Lady of Czestochowa

The magnetic attraction of Jasna Gora, its treasure and source of innumerable miracles for the past five centuries, is the Miraculous Portrait of Our Lady of Czestochowa. It was in her honor that the faithful erected a chapel, a beautiful church with numerous towers, and enshrined the priceless treasure. In a word, it was for her that they accomplished all that Jasna Gora ever was, is, or shall be. It is fitting then, that we too honor this story of the Miraculous Madonna of Czestochowa.

Based on Tradition

At the outset we must admit, that up to 1382 we have no concrete facts as to the origin and early history of this painting. For that, we rely on facts transmitted by popular belief and tradition among the faithful. This is the story we shall recount in detail.

Origin

The origin of this traditional painting traces back to that part of the Blessed Mother's life of which Marjan Gawalewicz speaks in his immortal "Legends." The Mother of God, he says, remained on earth alone in tears and with her sorrows. She enjoyed but two happy moments in her life, viz., when Jesus was born, and when, on the third day after His Resurrection, she saw Him alive. For fourteen years, she remained at the home of St. John leading a quiet, and a rather inconspicuous life, as befitted the chosen one of the Son of God. Her eyes, saturated with tears, were fixed on the earth which was marked with the stain of her Divine Son's blood. Although her heart was pierced by seven pangs of sorrow, and she lived wearing a veritable crown of thorns, in her pure heart there was no bitterness toward this world or its people. She was still their true friend, guardian and benefactress to the last moment of her earthly life. Even now, through all these centuries, she remains the same.

MOTHER OF THE SUFFERING

Heaven, with all its majesty, awaited her with regal splendor. In her compassion for the people, it was Mary who desired to remain with them, suffering and suppressing her sorrows because she was, to them, a consoling mother. Observing with tearful eyes, she saw the misery of her fellow creatures. She wanted to fathom and understand the suffering of the people so that from Heaven she could always remain the Mother of the oppressed on earth. Pensive in sufferings, with deep sorrow reflecting in her eyes and clouded brow, the Blessed Virgin passed through life just as the Evangelist St. Luke painted her image on a cypress table top: "free and pure from all earthly stain."

STORY OFTEN TOLD

Many writers have already told and retold the story of this portrait of the Blessed Mother. The fame of her exquisite beauty and virtuous life had spread far and wide, creating exceptional interest among the then living gentry. Among others, there is, preserved to this day, a document of St. Ignatius, Bishop of

Antioch, who later was martyred in defense of his faith. In a letter addressed to St. John the Apostle, he wrote: "If I may be worthy and deserving, my desire is to visit Jerusalem and see the saints living there, especially Mary, the spouse of St. Joseph, of whom it is said, 'She is an exceptional personality, one whose acquaintance everyone seeks. I ask you, who of our faith, if he is our friend, would not be overjoyed to see and speak with the one person who gave birth to the true God?"

The learned Dionesius, the Carthusian, writes that the faithful visited the home of St. John the Apostle in large numbers, led by a desire to see the Most Holy Virgin Mary. Other Christians who lived some distance away, not being able to visit Nazareth, were at least partially satisfied to have an image of the Mother of God amongst them. Thus Canisius writes (lib. 1 par.20), "When many people were desirous of seeing the Mother of God, those who were not able to go to her, satisfied their most ardent desires by keeping amongst them this immortal souvenir, which they passed on from one to another.

ST. LUKE, THE ARTIST

Following then popular demand and personal desires, a group of virgins assisted the Blessed Mother in Jerusalem, and under her guidance, formed the first congregation of women. They prevailed upon St. Luke, an accomplished artist, to make a portrait of the Blessed Mother. He made it on a table top at the home of St. John. At this table, the Blessed Mother usually sat doing her work. Of this fact we have the testimony of Sixtus of Sienna (Bib lib 2 lib 1); "St. Luke, after completing the life of Christ, with brush and paints made a portrait of His Blessed Mother." A Roman writer, Nicefar (lib 15c-14), adds this comment, "The portrait of the Blessed Mother St. Luke painted with his own hands. While she was still alive, she saw the painting and impressed into it the pleasing expression of her countenance."

THE MOTHER OF GOD

St. Epifanius, in the second book of Nicefar on Church history, writes, "At all times Mary was dignified, saying very little, speaking only when necessary; and in her own simple, pleasing and respectful manner, she was kind to all. In her stature, she was slightly above average. Her manner of expression was simple and understandable to all. Unruffled and serious, she was never seen to be angry. Her complexion was that of wheat, light hair, sharp eyes tinted with brown and olive colored pupils. Her eyebrows were somewhat drooped and appropriately tinted in black. Her nose was elongated; her blossoming lips full of sweet expression. She was not self-centered but sincere and forward — a lover of admirable humility. She was satisfied to dress according to native customs, as may be deduced from her headdress. In a word, she was filled with gratitude towards God, thankful for everything."

THE TABLE

Tradition gives us the following information about the table on which the portrait was painted. When the youthful Jesus lived with his mother and St. Joseph at Nazareth, He learned the art of carpentry under the expert guidance and watchful eye of His foster father. At times, He completed odd jobs and amongst the many things that Jesus built was this table, which He made for home use. When He died on the cross, the Blessed Mother moved to the home of St. John, her guardian, and amongst the personal belongings she took with her was this small piece of furniture upon which, later, the portrait was painted.

Is it possible to imagine a more elevating beginning for this portrait, a more supernatural origin of an object preserved intact to our day? Christ Jesus, with His hands — Divine, though child-like as yet — completed it giving us an inspiring example of the obligation everyone has in life to work. The Virgin Mary spent long hours working by this table, with a heart saddened by sorrow but elevated to Heaven in prayer and meditation. This table was touched every few minutes by those holy hands which nursed the God-Man. By its side, for hours, sat the Holy Mother of Sorrows, and as she wept, her tears soaked into the grain of this table as they fell upon it.

At last, through the intercession of the pious virgins of Jerusalem, this table fell into the hands of St. Luke, the artist, who for hours sat there admiring the sacred countenance of the Mother of God, immortalizing it with his art. While chatting with her, he gathered material from their conversation which later aided him in writing the gospels. Who, may we ask, could give better and more complete information about the mystery of the Annunciation, the birth of Christ, the flight into Egypt, the hidden life of Jesus or the early history of the Church, than His Blessed Mother, Mary, the Virgin?

MIRACULOUS PROVIDENCE OF GOD

This precious painting of the Mother of God survived through all the ages and changes of time. The miraculous providence of God watched over it and saved it from ruin and destruction during the siege of Jerusalem. Guided by God, the Christians left the city and hiding in the hills near a town called Pella, carried with them the painting of the Mother of Our Redeemer. For the first three centuries, this priceless souvenir was retained by the faithful in the East, especially at Jerusalem, and with special care it was concealed in the underground hideouts and catacombs.

ST. HELENA AND CONSTANTINE THE GREAT

In the year 326, St. Helena, the mother of Constantine the Great, burning with an ardent desire to locate the sacred relic, despite her advanced age and the difficulties of distant travel, went to Jerusalem and there with the help of God found the sacred souvenir. St. Helena, upon her arrival at Jerusalem, contacted the congregation of virgins, the old associates of the Blessed Mother. It was here that she found the painting under their vigilant and respectful care. This portrait, and a grand collection of other relics, she brought back and presented to her son, Constantine the Great, who at the time was building the capital of the Byzantine empire. According to the testimony of Nicefar (lib 18 cap 16) shortly after the council of Nice, the Emperor Constantine the Great, decided to erect a church at Constantinople near his palace and dedicated it to the Holy Name of Mary. In this church, he deposited the sacred painting. He called the city New Rome and chose the Mother of God as Patroness.

CONSTANTINOPLE SAVED

Within a very short time, the painting became famous throughout the entire vicinity because of the special graces received by all who prayed before it. The result was, that all respected it and paid it special homage. In the East, the successors of Emperor Constantine followed in his footsteps with extraordinary devotion to the Blessed Mother. When the Saracen tribes besieged the city, the painting of the Blessed Virgin was carried in solemn procession, by distinguished citizens and senators, through the streets of the city and around the dikes. The Saracens, seeing this, were greatly frightened and fled in dismay.

SAVED FROM DESTRUCTION

The sacred painting survived the reign of Emperor Izauryn who incited the people to a bitter hatred of holy objects and, as a result, thousands were destroyed by fire.

During those turbulent times, the painting was hidden in the very palace of the emperor by his wife, Irene, and daughter who remained faithful to the laws and teachings of the Holy Church. Respected by all, this painting was considered a priceless gift among the empresses. Thus, for example, Empress Irene gave it as a special gift to Eudoxia; Eudoxia gave it to Pulcheria and Pulcheria, in turn, gave it to her successor, etc. For five hundred years this sacred painting remained at the court of Constantine.

AMBASSADOR'S REPORT

Nichols Lanchoronski, the ambassador of King Sigismund August to the court of Constantinople, made a very profound and thorough investigation on the spot of the origin and history of this painting now at Czestochowa. He came to the convincing conclusion that the entire tradition of this painting is founded on certain and historical facts. Unfortunately, this document was lost.

AT BELZKI

It can be readily understood how the painting was brought into Russia from Constantinople; then to Halicia and finally to the castle of Belzki; because, as we know, the light of Christian faith spread from Constantinople through Bulgaria, Moravia, the Czech country and finally into Russia. The emperors of the eastern countries gave their daughters and sisters in marriage to the royalty of those countries and, as a dowry, gave this sacred painting.

It is an historical fact, that the Russian autocrats intermarried with the Polish royalty. For example, Mary Dobrogniewa, the daughter of Jarostaw, was the wife of Casimir I; Wislawa, a Russian, was the wife of Boleslaus II; Boleslaus II married Zdislawa; Boleslaus IV took unto himself Anastazja and, after her death, married Helena; Miecislaus III — Eudoxia; Leszek, the White, married Grzymislawa; Leszek, the Black — Gryfina. All of these were Russian princesses.

The Opolscy princes were inter-related with the Polish kings and their families through marriage. Ladislaus, an Opolski prince, substituted on the throne of Poland for Louis, king of Poland and

Hungary. Through the intermarriage of Russian royalty with those of Constantinople and later with the Polish royalty, this miraculous painting was brought to the castle of Belzki, where it remained for 500 years. Thus, Red Russia came into possession of this Miraculous Portrait.

During the reign of Casimir the Great, in the year 1352, the Ukraine, shattered and divided, was added to the Kingdom of Poland. Being a progressive and cultured ruler, Casimir immediately brought to the people of the Ukraine a higher standard of education and assured them, at the same time, of ample protection against their enemies. After his death, the people of Poland crowned Louis of Hungary as their ruler. Louis, however, spent most of his time on foreign soil and entrusted the destiny of Poland partially to his mother, Elizabeth, and partially to other relatives. Consequently, that part of Russia known as Red, came under the sceptre of Ladislaus, which up until then had been a palatinate of Hungary.

RECAPTURE

The uncertainty of the times gave rise to bloody struggles. Ladislaus, on ascending to the throne, was forced to fight to recapture all the castles from the Russian lords, including the castle of Belz. On capturing Belz, his first public act was to pay homage to the Miraculous Painting. Later, he ordered the portrait installed with great pomp and ceremony in a specially prepared chamber.

Unfortunately, not long after the official dedication, the castle of Belz was attacked and besieged by the Tartars. During the heat of battle, an arrow shot from the bow of a Tartar warrior, entered the chapel through one of the windows and struck the sacred painting, making a scar on the throat of the Virgin, a mark which to this day remains. Upon seeing the desecration of this sacred painting, Ladislaus, strengthened in spirit and inspired by a supernatural zeal, miraculously saved the day from total defeat.

This victory, however, did not ensure the future security of the painting because the Tartars came back and attacked almost constantly. To save the sacred portrait from total destruction, Ladislaus decided to transport the precious relic to the town of Opala, his birthplace, in Upper Silesia. The homeward journey carried him through Czestochowa, where night came upon him, so he decided to remain there until daybreak, depositing the precious painting for the night in a small wooden parish church under the patronage of the Assumption of Our Blessed Mother.

The following morning, under his personal supervision, the painting was placed in a wagon to be drawn away but, to the surprise of everyone, the horses could not move the carriage from its place. Greatly disturbed, the prince fell upon his knees before the image and, fervently praying, begged the Virgin for guidance as to what should be done with the portrait. His prayers were heard, for twice in a dream he received a special revelation to permanently deposit the portrait there in Czestochowa on Jasna Gora or Bright Hill. Ladislaus was convinced this was the will of God, so, in solemn procession, he brought the portrait into the Church of the Assumption.

All this actually happened on the Wednesday after the feast of St. Bartholomew on the 26th day of August in the year 1382.

THE CHURCH ON JASNA GORA OR BRIGHT HILL

Thus, on this very day, Ladislaus signed an official document ordering the erection on Jasna Gora of a convent, a church and a cloister, and financed the construction of these buildings himself.

THE PAULINE FATHERS

To preserve this sacred painting, Ladislaus was instrumental in bringing into Poland the Pauline Fathers from the Convent of Nosztre, Hungary, and to them he entrusted the care of this portrait. There may be a question in some minds as to just why Ladislaus imported religious monks from Hungary. The answer to this question is very simple. Ladislaus heard a great deal about this religious order of monks from his cousin, Louis of Hungary, who was one of the greatest benefactors of this order. He also knew them from personal contacts which he had made while touring Hungary. Since his desire was to place Poland's greatest treasure in competent and trustworthy hands, he called upon the monks of St. Paul to care for this sacred painting because, at that time, they were considered the most pious and religious in Europe. St. John of Capistrano, at that time, wrote the following about the Pauline Friars: "If anyone wishes to see angels in human flesh, he has to go only to the cloister of Nosztre in Hungary. There he can observe the daily life of the Pauline Fathers, and I assure you that he will be satisfied." Upon the invitation of Ladislaus, sixteen White Friars arrived. In all probability they were Slovenes, inasmuch as their speech could be understood by all the inhabitants. Since then, for the past five and one half centuries, the white Pauline habit has stood guard at Jasna Gora and is intimately connected with the history of the Miraculous Painting of Czestochowa.

THE SCARS

It can be easily noticed that on the face of the painting there are two scars. These were made by the Hussites in the year 1430. The other scar on the throat, as mentioned above, was made by a Tartar's arrow at the castle of Belz. The Blessed Mother desires these stigmas to remain forever on her sacred image. This is apparent from the fact that, during the reign of Jagiello, an artist engaged in retouching the painting, resorted to every known artistic means to efface them but to no avail; they always reappeared.

TWO DRESSES

For decorative purposes, the portrait has two dresses. One is composed of precious jewels; the other, beaded in rich colors. The jeweled ornament is practically priceless because in its construction may be found the richest contributions of all the families of Poland. The beaded dress, embroidered with beads on a golden cloth, is not too expensive, but treasured immensely because it is composed of beads assembled by peasant women. There was still another dress made of pearls, renowned for their size and shape; as for example, a pearl having the shape of a face, a heart or an egg. Included in this collection was the pearl of Constanty Sobieski, the king's son. Unfortunately, in 1909, this dress was torn off the altar and stolen by some thief. As a consequence of this theft, a movement was started to make a silver dress to replace the stolen treasure.

Every Holy Thursday these decorative dresses are interchanged on the sacred painting because, on that particular day, there are no devotions in the miraculous chapel. The ceremony is very elaborate. The fathers of the convent take down the Miraculous Painting and carry it into the treasure chamber. There, they strip it of the crown and decorations, clean all the jewels, then place a new dress on the painting. Amid solemn chant and fervent prayers, the painting is then carried in solemn procession and restored to its original place of honor. Any person, by simply coming in contact with this sacred image, admits that it produces a strange and lasting impression.

THE CROWN

The present crown of gold, decorated with jewels, is a gift of Pope Pius X who, in sympathy with the suffering nation, sent it as a gift from his paternal heart — a token of his love for the Polish people. The former crown was the gift of Pope Clement XI in 1717. Unfortunately, in 1909, it was stolen together with the dress. The crown of the painting, as one may notice upon closer scrutiny, is supported by two groups of angels.

CORONATION

The first official and public coronation of this painting took place in Poland in 1717. The ceremony was performed by Bishop Jan Krzystof Szembek. The celebration was very solemn, as the convent chronicle recalls. The crowd of pilgrims was so immense that some 148 thousand communicants received the Holy Eucharist. The second coronation took place in 1910 and attracted some one half million faithful to Jasna Gora. The act of coronation was performed by the Bishop of Wlaclaw, Stanislaus Zdzitowiecki. This, indeed, was the most solemn of all ceremonies ever to be observed on Jasna Gora.

BLACK MADONNA

It may be of interest to know why the face of the Blessed Mother on this painting is so dark, almost black. After much deliberation and research, the following conclusions were made: The portrait was painted by an individual who saw and knew the Mother of God. Even in the sacred scriptures, we find a description of the Blessed Mother's features, and to her the Church applies these words, "I am black but beautiful." (Cant Cant). Even though these words may be taken in the spiritual and metaphorical sense, they may be interpreted to mean the beauty of the body and the color of the face. Is this not exemplified in the portrait on Jasna Gora? Even though the painting is dark and almost black, is there another portrait of the Mother of God, more beautiful, more respected and revered, or a greater dispenser of graces and blessings than the Virgin of Jasna Gora or Bright Hill?

THE ARTIST

From a simple study of the painting, we can pick out the artist. A critical eye, for example, will readily tell us that a German's style of painting differs from that of a Frenchman or Italian. An Italian artist, again, has a different conception of beauty than a Pole, a Chinese differs from a Japanese. What may be the cause of this? The answer is simple. Since the Blessed Mother was not only the most holy of souls, without stain or scar of sin, she was also the most beautiful of all women. Any artist imagining her appearance, which he was to paint on the canvas, would take for a model the most beautiful woman he could find, and for the model he would take someone of his own race and nation, because love of one's nation and fatherland has a peculiar redundancy in the works of an accomplished artist. Thus it follows, that an Italian, painting a Blessed Virgin would generally present her as a plump figure, with fair complexion and black eyes and hair. A Frenchman paints in a similar style because a woman with such features and perfections is considered an acme of perfection and beauty among Italians and Frenchmen. On the other hand, a Hollander and a German would paint the Blessed Virgin with light hair, even slightly gilded blue eyes, and the face almost white tinted with shadows. A Pole would paint her with a white countenance even tinted with pink or red, bright eyes and blonde hair. In other words, an Italian will paint the most beautiful Italian woman; a Frenchman, the most beautiful French woman; a German, a German; a Pole, a Pole, etc. That is only natural. It is an historical fact that there was only one Mother of God. Some writers of the Church have given a description of her appearance. She was of Jewish origin, consequently, she surely had some Jewish features. The fact is that the painting at Jasna Gora embodies all of these features and characteristics, so it naturally follows that the one who painted the Virgin, knew her and was acquainted with her. Tradition comes to our aid explaining that this artist was none other than St. Luke.

THE COLOR

If the colors of the Virgin on the painting were light or even of a yellow tint, we could readily understand it. But, it is so dark that it is almost impossible to distinguish the features. The fact that it has existed for so many centuries partially explains this condition, inasmuch as a few ages are already ascribed to its existence. It was hidden away in various places which were far from ideal for the storage of works of art, especially paintings. For a few centuries, it was retained in the East where, to this day, there exists the following traditional custom. The faithful burn votive candles in front of sacred pictures and images. Consequently, dust and smoke do their share of destruction on the paintings. Furthermore, there also exists the custom of kissing pictures. This custom is so widespread among the people that it has now become almost a superstition. Those who fail to kiss a holy picture are said to have insulted it. Considering then the fact that this painting of the Virgin was held in great esteem and venerated by all, one can imagine how much abuse it must have undergone from constant handling and kissing. Again, it must be kept in mind that it is almost six centuries since the portrait was installed at Jasna Gora and the smoke from the innumerable candles constantly burning on the altars is more than sufficient cause to darken the painting. No small wonder then, that the painting, so old and so abused for centuries, is in such poor condition.

RESTORATION

In 1925, the Pauline Fathers, who are the authorized custodians of this sacred relic, created a special commission. This commission was sanctioned by the Polish hierarchy. Their aim was to examine the painting and, if it was found necessary, to have it restored by an artist of their choice. To accomplish the task, the special board entrusted this honorable and important mission to Prof. John Rutkowski, the first director and custodian of fine arts at Warsaw. Prof. Rutkowski was a famous figure in the world of ecclesiastical art and was known especially for his restoration of Reuben's painting, "Descent from the Cross" which was placed in the art gallery at Kalisz.

Prof. Rutkowski began the work on this sacred treasure with the greatest sense of responsibility and piety and we must admit that the fulfillment of his mission was praiseworthy. The actual work, or restoration lasted from November, 1925 to March, 1926.

The renovated painting was then restored to its original place of honor in the main altar.

SIZE

The actual painting, without frames, is 122.2 centimeters high (approx. 19 in.), 82.2 cm. wide (approx. 13 in.) and 3.5 cm. thick (approx. 1/2 in.). The background is composed of three boards joined together. The paints used in the painting of the features of the Blessed Mother and Child Jesus have a resin base.

Since its installation on Jasna Gora, the painting has been renovated twice. The first time in 1430 during the reign of Jagiello after it was partially destroyed by the Hussites. The second restoration took place in 1682 during the reign of King John Sobieski. Unfortunately, the second renovation consisted of a partial repainting, a deed befitting neither the original nor the dignity of the painting.

ORIGINAL COLOR

At that time, it was necessary to bring out its original colors. After restoring it to its original state, it was found that the cape and dress of the Blessed Mother had a sort of granite color, decorated with a golden design in the shape of lilies. The lining of the cape was of a carmine color with a golden border. The Child Jesus was vested in a dress of shaded carmine, decorated with designs of lilies, rosettes and clusters of three leaves, finished in a sort of dull gilt.

The face and hands of the Blessed Mother are of a bronze shade, the eyes somewhat narrow, an elongated nose, a small mouth and heavy set lips made prominent by light shadings, especially in the upper part. On the left side of the face may be seen large clusters of falling hair ending under the cape. Outstanding are two prominent scars on the right cheek of the Blessed Mother, running parallel to the middle, fading softly toward the neck. The scar on the neck, mentioned above, was caused by a sharp and pointed arrow, viz., the arrow of a Tartar warrior.

The face and hands of the Child Jesus are of the same color composition as those of the Blessed Mother. The head is decorated with curly hair. The aureole above the head of the Blessed Mother and the Child Jesus is made up of soft rays, running in all directions, breaking above the evenness of the portrait.

The surface of the back side of this painting was covered with cloth. Here may be detected scenes and designs depicting the history of the painting. Here also are listed some of the miracles performed through the intercession of the Madonna of Czestochowa.

After the restoration of 1925, the dress no longer rested immediately on the bare wood of the painting. Since the old practice was found to injure the painting itself, it was wisely decided to leave a small air space between the painting and the specially constructed shield to which the dress is attached.

From the time when the Miraculous Painting was first deposited on Jasna Gora, it has been exported from Czestochowa on three different occasions, and it has been twice removed from Jasna Gora to the Church of St. Barbara. The first time, it was brought to Cracow for the purpose of restoration and general repairs. Twice it was brought to Upper Silesia when the convent was in danger and there was fear that the Miraculous Painting would be desecrated. Once, it was deposited at the settlement of Glosgow and, another time, in the vicinity of Lublin.

On summarizing the above mentioned facts, everyone must understand the maternal solicitude which the Mother of God has towards the inhabitants of Jasna Gora. For 90 years before the sacred painting was brought to Czestochowa, those poor people were separated from their mother country as a result of the invasion of the Czechs. However, the Mother of God, solicitous for them and desiring to have her motherly eyes upon them, turned to them. This was a sign that even though they were separated from their country, the Mother of God would watch over them.

After the first World War, when the fate of Silicia hung in the balance, the Poles living in the vicinity of Jasna Gora made special pilgrimages to Czestochowa. It was here that they received new strength and inspired with the traditional Polish spirit, were victorious in the plebiscite of 1921. It was the Madonna of Czestochowa that rejoined this part of Poland to the motherland.

MIRACLES AT CZESTOCHOWA

THE TERRIBLE INCIDENT AT LUBLIN

The gruesome tragedy of 1540 left an indelible imprint on the minds and spirit of the inhabitants of Lublin some few miles from Jasna Gora.

There lived a man, a butcher by trade, who was the owner and operator of a large slaughter house. Marcin Lanio and his wife, Malgorzata, enjoyed a rather prosperous life in company with their two sons, Piotrus, who was four, and Kazimierz, age two.

TRAGEDY

It happened one day that Marcin, accompanied by his helper, went to town on a shopping tour. The mother was preoccupied in the kitchen, preparing batter for bread which she was about to bake. As it happened, she ran short of yeast, so she left the house momentarily to borrow some from one of her neighbors. The two youngsters were left alone at home.

Piotrus, the older of the two, who on many occasions had seen the butchers slaughter the livestock in the yard, decided to imitate them. In his childish mind, he figured that the most convenient victim would be little Kazio, sleeping innocently in a nearby crib. Without much forethought, he took a large, sharp knife and slashed the throat of his sleeping infant brother. Seeing the flow of blood, he soon realized that something terrible had happened. He was overcome with fear of punishment and hid inside the large baker's oven left open by the absent housewife. Within a matter of moments, the unsuspecting mother, having returned and not hearing the children, thought them to be asleep. Consequently, she went about with her baking and started a log fire in the prepared oven. All of a sudden the blood froze in her veins as she heard the agonizing screams of her son, Piotrus, now helpless in the depths of the burning oven. Frantically, she pulled him out, but, it was too late. Piotrus, her son, had suffocated in the smoke-filled chamber and now she held his lifeless form in her arms.

As she looked about, paralyzed by this sudden turn of events, her staring eyes were fixed on another gruesome sight. She saw, in the blood soaked crib, the lifeless body of her younger son — dead. Shocked, she stood there staring and then, as consciousness returned, became completely demented, striking her head against the wall, pulling her hair and finally tearing her clothes to shreds. In her condition, she looked like a ghost from another world.

It was then that Marcin, her husband, returned home. He did not stop to think. As he saw the condition of his wife between the two corpses of his sons, he took an axe and crushed her skull with one blow.

REACTION

His mind cleared after a little while and he realized what had been done. Dreadful fear and remorse seized his body and soul. His mind, however, became enlightened by a sudden Heavenly impulse. He did not submit to despair but listened to the advice of pious friends and neighbors. He placed his entire and unshaken faith in Mary of Jasna Gora; she would not forsake him at this critical moment. He felt then and there, that the Madonna of Czestochowa to whom he was always so devoted would give the family back to him.

All the neighbors, by now mostly out of curiosity, assembled at the scene of the tragedy. Their surprise was augmented by the scene which followed. Marcin Lanio, without a word, loaded the three blood-soaked corpses into a wagon, and with the sign of the cross, turned the horses in the direction of Czestochowa. The bystanders watched this gruesome and tragic scene, some in fear, others in tears. This, indeed, was a public act of faith!

THE JOURNEY

In silence Marcin continued his hopeful journey through narrow roads, shaded by overhanging branches. The sides of the road were lined with a great number of skeptical people. Some of them, in amazement, wondered what prompted this man to be transporting three corpses in an open wagon. Many questioned his sanity and what he intended to do, since they knew that normally once the dead are dead, they so remain.

Marcin paid no heed to them because his mind and heart were focused on the Blessed Mother. He continued the pilgrimage in silent prayer fortified by unshaken confidence. Then, he saw in the distance, the shining cross on the cloister steeple. As the journey continued, he soon heard the sound of evening bells calling the faithful to prayer. His spirit was suddenly refreshed as the horses began to gallop and his prayer became more fervent and confident.

AT THE CHURCH

Finally, he arrived at the church and, with the help of some understanding bystanders, carried the three corpses in improvised caskets into the chapel. He himself did not enter because he had neither strength nor courage; but he lay prostrate before the main door. In tears he kissed the feet of the faithful as they entered the chapel and begged them to pray and intercede for his family before the throne of the Miraculous Madonna of Czestochowa.

THE MIRACLE

By now, it was dark in the rear of the chapel but the portrait of the Black Madonna, high above the main altar, took on a Heavenly splendor. The Blessed Sacrament was exposed on the altar and Blessed Stanislaw Oporowski, a pious and devout priest was conducting Benediction services. He too, joined in public supplication begging for mercy towards the unfortunate husband and father. As if inspired by some supernatural impulse, all the people in the Church added their suppliant voices. The crescendo of their tearful prayers mounted to near hysteria as they all sang the magnificent hymn to the Blessed Mother — the Magnificat. The atmosphere seemed to be so impregnated with some supernatural feeling that all hearts of the assembled stopped momentarily in the expectancy of something out of the ordinary. The moment did arrive! As they sang out the words of the hymn, "Because He that is mighty hath done great things to me and Holy is His Name," a sudden shock paralyzed the surprised congregation. Suddenly, the three dead people, up to this moment lifeless corpses, came to life and slowly rose from their resting place into the outstretched arms of the trusting and God-fearing father and husband.

THANKSGIVING

For a moment, silence which seemed to last an age, filled the edifice. Then, the outburst of spontaneous voices almost burst open the walls of the structure, as all joined in a hymn of thanksgiving to the Blessed Madonna of Czestochowa. Prominent among them were the voices of the once dead children and their resurrected mother.

Soon the fame of this miracle became worldwide and the emperor ordered a true copy of this Miraculous Portrait to be made and placed in the Cathedral in Vienna.

RESCUE AT SEA

In 1537, after many months at sea replete with the hardships and difficulties usual to seafaring men, a ship finally turned its bow towards Polish soil.

THE STORM

Suddenly, as often happens to this day in the Baltic Sea, an unexpected storm sprung up from almost nowhere. It seemed that all the vicious elements conspired to destroy the weather-beaten little craft and the weary crew. Mountainous waves all but swamped the creaking vessel. The howling winds, of hurricane proportions, smashed the main mast to splinters and tore all the sails to shreds.

The helpless and partially water-filled ship was being carried by the tide towards the Russian shores. Terrorized, everyone on board saw the approaching and inevitable destruction on the jagged rocks protruding from the whirling water. The dark sky and raging sea added to the fear of the weary travelers as night covered the horrible scene with its deathly pallor. Lightning made the sight more gruesome as, from time to time, it tore open the dark heavens above with long streaks of flashing light and cast ghostly shadows on the troubled sea.

Even the most experienced seamen, let alone the casual traveler, were in mortal fear. All, without exception, prepared for the final moment of destruction which seemed inevitable.

TURN TO GOD

Among the passengers of this helpless ship was a native of Poland, Stanislaw Laski, a knight of the Holy Sepulchre. Sensing the helplessness of the situation, he knew that only a miracle could save them from the approaching doom. When the most critical moment seemed to have arrived, he fell on his knees on the tilted deck and in a loud voice which could be heard above the din of the storm, he began to call to Our Lady of Czestochowa for help.

HELP ARRIVES

The mention of the Blessed Mother's name was like oil poured upon the troubled waters. As if by magic, the storm abated and the gigantic waves disappeared. All became quiet and serene. The star of the sea appeared; skies were bright and clear without a threatening cloud. Slowly then, the ship turned towards its haven.

ANOTHER INCIDENT

We are told that on a different occasion this same knight, Stanislaw Laski, was traveling on the Mediterranean Sea from Alexandria to Constantinople. Again, he found himself in the midst of a terrific storm. The ship took a terrible beating from the disturbed elements, and after the masts were broken and sails torn to bits, the craft was wrecked on the reef and sank. All the passengers were thrown into the raging sea.

In darkness, the knight and all the unfortunate voyagers floated around blindly. Finally, he grew weaker and could not stay afloat. His position seemed hopeless, so again he turned to Our Lady of Czestochowa, begging for help.

A FLOAT

With all his ebbing strength, he gathered together his senses and made a perfect act of faith with a solemn promise to the Blessed Mother that if she rescued him from his terrible predicament, he would make a special pilgrimage of thanksgiving to Jasna Gora. Struggling with the enraged elements and applying the last ounce of his strength, he suddenly felt a large piece of wood under him. He grabbed it and held on as he was picked up by a huge wave and safely deposited on the shore.

Not long after this miraculous incident, Stanislaw Laski arrived in Jasna Gora, grateful to Our Lady of Czestochowa.

BURNING AT THE STAKE

In 1623, there lived in Tikno, Prussia, the family of Marcin and Malgorzata Pokrzewinski and their little daughter, Zosia. They were members of the Baptist Church and firm followers of its teachings and beliefs.

CONVERSION

Being of moderate means, they had one servant girl who happened to be a devout Catholic. Little Zosia was very much attached to her and in their frequent associations she often asked about the Catholic faith, the sacraments, and especially the Blessed Mother. The good servant instructed Zosia privately, knowing all the while that her parents would object. It seemed that during their talks, when conversation turned to the subject of the Blessed Mother, their discussions were most enjoyable. The interest in the accomplishments and personality of the Blessed Lady grew to such proportions that Zosia became interested in forsaking her heretical belief and finally became a Catholic. When the parents learned of her conversion, they became furious — as could be expected under the circumstances.

At first, they attempted to bribe their child with promises if she renounced her new faith, but to no avail. Zosia, deep down in her heart, knew that she possessed the most precious gem; she possessed the one, true, Catholic faith. To her, there was no earthly gown as beautiful as the scapular of the Blessed Mother around her neck. All the promises of earthly gems, dresses and gowns could not change her mind.

The parents realized that tactics of leniency and benevolent promises were not producing the desired effect, so they became more severe and demanding.

PERSECUTION

The first act was to isolate her from the rest of the family by holding Zosia a prisoner in a special chamber. They beat her frequently; they even tried to change her convictions by starvation, but again to no avail. In the meantime, our little heroine did not despair or even falter for a moment in her faith. She constantly prayed to the Blessed Mother of Czestochowa, about whose blessings and solicitude she had heard so much from the servant girl. Very often she would repeat an act of consecration to the Madonna of Jasna Gora while praying for strength and perseverance.

One day, the parents, as a last resort, went to the place of her solitary confinement. On their knees, they pleaded with the little girl to renounce her Catholic faith. But, reinforced by some supernatural strength, Zosia would not submit to the parents' plea. Instead, she firmly responded: "My beloved parents, it is not I who should renounce what you call an error, but it is you who have renounced the true faith of Christ Jesus and embraced heresy."

She then dropped to her knees and pleaded and begged them to join her in professing the Catholic faith. Inflamed by some satanic rage and hatred, they pushed her aside with a warning, that from this very moment all mercy and love towards her was gone, and that because of her stubbornness she would pay with her life.

CONDEMNATION

The family then met in judgement and unanimously agreed that the "Papist" must be put to death by burning at the stake, thus suffering the just end of a heretic, according to the then existing customs among the Baptists in Poland. The following morning, on the day of the appointed execution, many Baptists gathered together to see the expiation of the little girl. Zosia was brought forward at a given signal and walked without a sign of fear but rather, her countenance was resplendent with a certain smile of satisfaction.

Walking forward, silently murmuring prayers to the Blessed Mother, she reminded the bystanders of those scenes which were enacted during the bloody days of Nero's persecutions. Those more sensitive and unbiased wept silently at the pitiful sight. To the perverted parents however, the serene stature and complacent attitude of the little lady was a cause of greater hatred towards her.

EXECUTION

Wood was gathered together and stacked into a high pyre and the father prepared to light it with a burning torch. In the meantime, Zosia fell on her knees and in a loud voice, so that all could hear, commended her soul to God. Then, the relatives roughly threw her high up on top of the prepared altar of sacrifice.

There she stood, upright and straight as a true martyr of Christ, and called out, "O Lady of Czestochowa, be my protectress." She fixed her eyes towards Heaven as though she was staring at someone. The torch was then put to the pyre. Instantly, with a resounding flash, the entire stake was enveloped in raging flames, the dense smoke rising like a giant column towards the sky completely shielding the figure of the martyr from the view of the witnesses.

In joyful expectancy, the heretics stood by with strained ears, awaiting the inevitable painful outcries and moaning of the prepared victim. But all that could be heard, was the crackling of the burning timbers.

THE MIRACLE

After the smoke subsided, all that could be seen were the remains of the burning charred wood which was still glowing and, in the very center, the untouched and unharmed erect figure of the little martyr with eyes fixed on the heavens above.

The Blessed Mother came to the aid of her small follower. She enveloped the saintly girl in her protective cloak and thus miraculously saved her from burning. As proof of the miracle,

Zosia had a slight burn on her side. Seeing this, the gawking bystanders suddenly began to run away, screaming at the top of their frightened voices: "Witchcraft, those are spells and charms of the Catholics." The startled parents, still doubtful as to the reality and veracity of this miracle, withdrew the sentence of death, but continued to persecute little Zosia.

After suffering the most diabolical and depressing treatment at the hands of her parents, the girl finally succeeded in running away from this unfortunate home. Having no other place of refuge, she went to Jasna Gora. It should be noted here, likewise, that from birth, Zosia had a definite defect in her speech and she stuttered quite noticeably.

ANOTHER MIRACLE

Upon entering the chapel at the shrine, she stood before the Miraculous Portrait and began to weep bitterly recalling, at this moment, the miraculous escape from burning under the tender care of the Blessed Mother for whom she was willing to die. Then, she had another cause for gratitude. She noticed that her life-long defect of speech was gone as she began to pray in a loud, clear, and normal voice.

Sophie Pokrzewinska gave solemn testimony to the above, before eyewitnesses, who testified to the truth of her statements. One of the portraits on the wall of the shrine in Czestochowa is, to this day, a silent witness to this miracle.

A SICK MOTHER

In the vicinity of Tarnov, the territory often called "Little Poland" or "The Blacksmith Shop of Saints," lived a certain Anna Mycielska in 1603. After contracting some mysterious disease, she suffered excruciating pain and misery for eight months. The continuous suffering, for which there was no relief, so depressed the unfortunate woman that she begged God to graciously allow her to die.

The husband and five children could no longer bear the sight of their mother going through such intense suffering. The doctors, try as they might, could find no antidote. Amid this turmoil, the family decided to bring their Anna to the Shrine of Our Lady of Czestochowa.

THE PILGRIMAGE

They placed her in a carriage and began their journey as slowly as possible because every jolt and bump added to the misery of the sick woman. Accompanied by the husband and children, the pitiful entourage finally reached their destination.

It was early morning when, in the bright reflection of the rising sun, the group of pilgrims carried their mother and wife on an improvised stretcher into the chapel. The faithful had just begun to arrive and some candles were lit before the altar. The Miraculous Portrait of the Madonna was still hidden behind a silver veil when they placed before the altar the pain-torn form of the sick woman wrapped in blankets. A heartbreaking scene it was, just like the one described in the Gospel where the sick, to reach Our Lord Jesus, had to be dropped on stretchers through openings in the roof tops.

Soon, it seemed the world changed about them as they were awakened to the full realization of their presence in the shrine by the echo of the morning hymn as it was intoned somewhere in the distant choir loft. They fell on their knees and, prostrate before the stretcher of the sick woman, prayed as never before begging God Almighty for help and a cure for this unfortunate victim. Poor Anna stared blankly at the altar — being devoid of all consciousness and feeling because of frequent convulsions.

THE CURE

Suddenly, the Miraculous Portrait was unveiled and the blessed Mother appeared in all her magnificence and beauty. It was then that the sick woman arose from her litter, miraculously cured, fully conscious and free from all pain. She dropped to her knees in thanksgiving, praising the Blessed Mother for her kindness and solicitude.

The happy family remained at the shrine for three days in appreciation for God's goodness to them and then, on foot, returned home to lead a normal life.

SOLEMN TESTIMONY

The following testimony was given before witnesses and under oath on June 14, 1720 by a certain Michal Pruszynski, the Canon of Kijow, pastor of Toporow, in the diocese of Luch, in the deanery of Bielski.

LAST WILL AND TESTAMENT

"I owe my vocation to the priesthood to the Blessed Mother. I served her to the best of my God-given ability all my life. I have been endowed by God with a frail constitution and questionable health. Towards the end of 1717, I began to grow gradually weaker and, after two years of suffering with a very serious illness, I was completely paralyzed. I became deaf and blind; I was almost like a living corpse, so I asked my confreres to prepare my coffin and have my grave dug out. I made my last will and testament on February 8, 1720 in the presence of Fathers Peter Markowski, Peter Brozowski, and Jakob Kruszewski. The above-mentioned witnesses tell me I died later the same day.

DEATH

They placed me in the prepared casket dressed in my alb. With the cover closed, I was then carried to an adjacent dark room and left there all afternoon in extreme freezing cold. Normally,

I should have frozen completely. I remember that it was then, that St. Paul, the venerable old Patriarch of the Pauline Fathers, whose feast we commemorated on January 10, appeared to me. He took me by the right and said, 'Arise and go pay your respects to the Madonna of Czestochowa — because it is by her grace and intercession that you are arising from the dead.' When he disappeared with the words, 'Jesus and Mary of Czestochowa,' I began to call for help.

RESURRECTION

The turmoil that followed was almost indescribable. Some fled, others frantically pulled on the boards sealing my casket. When I arose, I asked first for the grand old Patriarch who ordered me to arise. He was gone. Then I realized that I had spent a whole day in freezing cold, dressed only in a thin alb — but, at the same time, my body was warm and normal in every respect. Despite all advice to the contrary, I was determined that even if I had to die on the way, I would leave immediately to thank the Madonna of Jasna Gora and thus fulfill the command of my benefactor.

PILGRIMAGE

Finally, after travelling a distance of 70 miles, I arrived on Jasna Gora on the 13th of April and, without help or assistance, I climbed the stairs to the convent. I often retold these wonderful events in my life but for more definite proof of their veracity, I now repeat them before witnesses."

Upon his return to the parish, he bought a beautiful portrait of Our Lady of Czestochowa and placed it in the church. Before this shrine many of his parishioners received untold graces and blessings.

THE PENETRATING EYES

It happened in the year 1672. There was a certain Turk, named Klater, who happened to be in Czestochowa on personal business. Despite the fact that he had made Poland his permanent home, and considered himself a Pole, he refused, time and again, to renounce his Mohammedan convictions and become a Catholic like the rest of the Polish people.

One day he was enjoying himself in the famous shrine city of Poland and, urged on by friends although moved more by personal curiosity, he visited Jasna Gora. The heavenly and majestic splendor of the interior decoration of the large church almost paralyzed him with admiration and awe. But, when he entered the miraculous chapel and looked into the holy countenance of Mary on the Miraculous Portrait, he was completely carried away. His heart was filled with a feeling hitherto unknown to him, and the understanding motherly eyes of Our Lady of Czestochowa looked down into his heart with a tenderness which he could not describe. In that steady, tender gaze, his soul was enveloped. Never before did he experience such emotion.

INSPIRATION

After a while, he looked around at the assembled people and, as he saw them all kneeling and praying, he was seized by an unexplainable force. Then, his knees were bent by a strength he could not resist and suddenly, he found himself joined with all the others in simple but humble prayer. Some extraordinary power within him seemed to be forcing his very lungs to expand and he wanted to cry out aloud.

UNDERSTANDING

Still those eyes of the Madonna stared at him, even though they seemed so gentle, they were penetrating and commanding.

What do they want from him? What does that Lady with the Child in her arms want from him? He does not know her at all, but ah, how he would like to know her. At last, a sigh of relief escapes his lips. Now he knows what she wants, as he is blinded by a flash of light from those fixed eyes. Suddenly, his beclouded mind was illumined — the Madonna of Jasna Gora wants him to know that due to the fact he knows her not — he could know her now. Yes, that is exactly what she wants and it is this message that those eyes are trying to convey to him. He then fell prostrate on the floor, offering sincere thanks and salutations. Suddenly, as if led by an invisible hand, he went in search of someone, in fact anyone, who could give him more information about her.

INFORMATION

Friendly bystanders led him to the Abbot who happened to be the very pious and highly respected Augustyn Kordecki. The venerable priest inquired as to the purpose of his unexpected visit and Klater, with folded hands, fell on his knees and said, "Tell me, Father, all about this Holy Lady in the Portrait; I want to be her servant and be devoted to her for the rest of my life." With paternal solicitude and care, the good priest prepared him for baptism and gave him the necessary information about the Catholic faith.

BAPTISM

On the appointed day, sometime later, the candles were lit on the altar and the chapel filled to capacity with devout worshippers. The morning hymn was sung as usual as all the heads bowed in solemn prayer and a slight ripple of sound floated over the audience. At this moment, the usual unveiling of the Miraculous Portrait took place. Then, Father Augustyn Kordecki administered the Sacrament of Baptism to the Turk and gave him the name of Urban. Everyone was touched to the very soul by this sight, as the neophyte, vested in white, was led to the altar. His countenance reflected heavenly joy because he came to know his Lady and

Queen. Now he was her child! Her faithful servant to whom he gave his heart. He fell on his knees and again, as before, those most blessed eyes stared at him. But now everything was different because the mother and the son understood each other as he laid his devout heart at her feet and, in return, she assured him of all the graces with her blessings.

Thus, Urban Klater, remained a faithful and devoted servant among the children of Mary.

THE LOST HORSEMAN

In the courtyard of Zygmunt III, King of Poland, lived Dominik Koniwerski with his devoted wife, Maryanna. His duties consisted in caring for the King's horses.

In 1641, he wandered away from the castle and disappeared as though into thin air. Naturally, his wife was greatly upset. For three months, there was no sign of the missing horseman. The passing of time was a nightmare for the anxious spouse as she prayed and hoped for his safe return. In all her prayers, Maryanna constantly and hopefully placed her husband under the protection of Our Lady of Czestochowa.

On sleepless night, as she continued to pray with greater fervor than ever before, Our Lady of Czestochowa appeared before her, indescribably beautiful, and in a sweet voice said to her, "Do not fear, your husband is living; you will see him soon; but you must place the Rosary on which you salute me on my painting in Czestochowa as a memento." After saying this, the Blessed Virgin disappeared. Thus it happened that, the very next day, the husband returned home in perfect health. The wife immediately went to Jasna Gora to place her rosary beads at the miraculous shrine at Czestochowa, in accordance with the wishes of Our Lady.

THE FIRE

In the village of Sierodz, about the year 1598, there lived the rather well-to-do and hard-working family of Christopher Godziszewski. Early one evening, after a hard day's work, the tired family retired to bed as usual.

During the night a fire broke out in the dwelling, but the tired people slept so soundly that even the crackling of the burning timbers did not arouse them. The villagers, awakened by the reflection of the flames in the sky and the gushing smoke, gathered around the house and stood by helplessly as they watched, with horror, the enveloping flames reducing the proud earthly belongings of the Godziszewskis to ashes.

The unfortunate family within, unaware of the catastrophe, slept soundly until awakened by the fumes of the smoke. Seeing the fire surrounding them, with all avenues of escape closed and inevitable death staring them in the face, they soon made their decision. The father and the family gathered together in the very heart of this burning inferno, fell on their knees and with sincere and trusting hearts offered themselves to the care of the Blessed Virgin.

THE MIRACLE

Suddenly, a miracle happened. the flames diminished and subsided so that the whole family walked out to safety through a veritable tunnel of fire between two walls. Just as unexpectedly, a sudden squall sprung up accompanied by torrential rains which soon extinguished the roaring flames.

Thus, the Blessed Mother, in her solicitude, saved the Godziszewski family from certain death and spared the rest of the village from a possible catastrophe.

THE MEDAL OF OUR LADY

It is a known fact, that the gallant knights of the Poland of old never appeared without a medal of Our Lady of Czestochowa suspended around their neck. Andrew Jezowski, a colonel, was no exception.

In 1677, it happened to be his duty to lead a small army of 1,500 men, against 10,000 Turks and Tartars in a combined force at the battle of Wojnilowa. Fortunes of war turned against him and he was taken captive. He was exposed to the most inhuman treatment and torture. Besides being starved and insulted, he was scourged three times a week, receiving 25 lashes each time.

When his executioners disrobed him for the first time, they found the medal on his chest. Greatly enraged and cursing terribly, they tore the sacred image from his neck. Then, to desecrate it even more, they threw it under the feet of the horses in the stable. In vain were his tears and entreaties for the return of his greatest treasure. Instead of returning the medal, the infidels inflicted more punishment and, after a merciless beating, they threw him on a cot in the prison cell.

THE PROTECTOR

In times of trouble or distress, he always held on to his medal but now it was gone. He prayed with all his heart to Our Lady of Czestochowa, begging her for the privilege of seeing the sacred image. Hardly had he finished praying, when he noticed that his old medal was beside him on the cot. With tears of joy moistening his cheeks, he immediately kissed the sacred image and placed it back around his neck.

One of the Tartar guards, seeing him venerate the medal, was greatly incensed and, cursing violently, tried to tear the medal away. Fortunately, one of the senior guards stepped in and, restraining the attempts of the junior Tartar, said: — "Let this unhappy creature pay homage to his mother as we do to ours." After this episode, no one ever tried to take the medal away.

In the meantime, under the special care of the Blessed Mother, the colonel was miraculously freed from prison and returned to Warsaw where he related the whole incident to King John III and his senators.

THE COLONEL'S ARMOR

In 1672, Sir Adam Strzalkowski, accompanied by a group of trustworthy witnesses, arrived at Jasna Gora and testified as follows:

"While fighting under King John Sobieski, I was cut off from the main army and taken prisoner by the enemy. One of the blood-thirsty Tartars raised his sword ready to strike me. Realizing, at this moment, that death was staring me in the face, I held on to my medal of Our Lady of Czestochowa which I always carry on my person. I begged her for help and protection and, with a most fervent and sincere prayer, I entrusted myself to her care.

THE STRANGE FORCE

Lo and behold! A miracle took place at that very moment; the Tartar's hands began to shake and quiver so that he could not raise the sword which then dropped to the ground. Perplexed by this sudden weakness and not knowing it cause, he began to pretend that his intention was merely to scare me and the other prisoners but that he would spare my life."

After a short while, the fierce Tartar, again overcome with hateful madness, raised the sword to behead his captive. This second attempt was also in vain because now, as before, his hand began to tremble. Growing weak, he dropped the sword harmlessly to the ground. Then he became extremely frightened because he understood the interference of some mysterious force which would not permit him to harm the captive. Therefore, he set him free.

Adam Strzalkowski then returned home to his native land but somehow could not stay and soon returned to another war against the infidel Turk to defend his fatherland.

✧✧✧✧

THE STOPPED BULLET

It happened in the battle of Cudno that a direct bullet hit him in the vicinity of his heart. He saw it coming; he felt and heard the impact on his breastplate but was not thrown from his horse. With his hand, he felt the spot and noticed a pierced hole in the armor but felt no pain, so he continued fighting.

After the battle, he began to investigate what actually happened to that bullet. This is what he found. The bullet penetrated the steel armor and was stopped by a medal of Our Lady of Czestochowa which was dented. Then, it fell harmlessly to the ground.

Seeing this, both he and all his friends, as eyewitnesses of this miracle, paid homage to Our Lady of Czestochowa.

THE REFLECTED LIGHT

One of the pious customs, preserved among the people from Slask, were the frequent pilgrimages made on foot to Jasna Gora. One of those was in progress sometime in 1672. Prompted by curiosity rather than devotion, a certain young lady, who was a Lutheran by religious conviction, joined the company of pilgrims. Her name was Martha. As the tireless pilgrims proceeded on their merry way through towns and villages, she refused to take part in any prayers or even the singing of the pious hymns because she was hardened in her heretical convictions.

CATASTROPHE

After some days of continuous traveling, the pilgrims came within sight of the distant spires reflecting in the bright rays of the sun. Moved with emotion and overcome to the very essence of their souls, they fell prostrate on the dusty road in solemn respect for the holy temple and abode of the Blessed Mother. With tearful eyes, they prayed with great fervor, praising God and Mary for their goodness. During this touching scene of public adoration, Martha stood as erect as a soldier at attention and, deep down in her heart, laughed at the pilgrims considering them absolute fools. By doing this, she thought in her perverted mind, that she would show her superiority.

But then, lo and behold!, a sudden flash of light reflected from the distant steeple and struck her as though it were a streak of lightning, throwing her to the ground. The frightened pilgrims rushed to her, and after a long time, using every known means of resuscitation, succeeded in bringing her back to normal consciousness.

RECOVERY

Having recovered, she admitted to them her mocking thoughts and personal pride as she stood there looking down with scorn upon those who knelt down to pray. Then it was, she explained to them, that from the heavenly light which struck her and effected such a change in her mind and heart, she now began to see clearly how stubborn and blinded she had been in heresy.

The pilgrimage continued acquiring a new Catholic member because from that very moment Martha felt convinced about the reality of our Catholic faith. Upon arrival at Jasna Gora, the young lady made her profession of faith and, inspired by the beautiful Madonna on the portrait of Czestochowa, became one of her most devout and ardent admirers.

RELIGIOUS WAR

Many and extremely bloody were the religious battles and wars of the middle ages. In 1617, Mansfield, a great figure in the past military history of Germany, at the head of a powerful array, besieged the town of Glewice in Slask. He was a deadly enemy of the emperor of Rome and now commanded a powerful unit of Lutheran armies.

The Catholic forces, ill-equipped and numbering but a small detachment of enlisted men, were stationed in the besieged city. Humanly speaking, it appeared impossible that they could resist successfully the invading armies. Everything seemed to point to complete ruin and utter destruction.

In this terrible predicament, their only hope was to seek help from Heaven. Thus, all the priests, officers, and soldiers together with the inhabitants of the town turned to Our Lady of Czestochowa for assistance and guidance. This was nothing new to them because these people residing in the vicinity of Slask were greatly devoted to the Blessed Mother.

Solemnly they consecrated the town of Glewice and themselves to the Queen of Heaven with a promise, that if it be the wish of God for them to be saved from their enemies, the entire population of the town would visit the shrine in Czestochowa.

This is what happened as recorded later in the annals of Czestochowa.

APPARITION

As they were nearing the completion of their suppliant prayers and began to return to the battle stations, the town was darkened. They saw high above in the sky, Our Lady of Czestochowa and, with her outspread cloak, she covered the whole town as if trying to shield it.

New courage and joy filled the depressed hearts of the suppliant people, as they watched the vision above them. In the enemy camp of the heretics, the fear and turmoil which followed was almost indescribable. Seeing Our Lady of Czestochowa appearing above her children, the frightened enemy fled in confusion, shouting at the top of their voices, "Glewice is under the protection of the Great Heavenly Lady; in vain are all our endeavors."

In the happy village there was a holiday decorum as the people filed into the churches, to the tune of tolling church bells, ever grateful to their defendress. Soon after, all those who were able, went to Czestochowa to fulfill their solemn promise to Mary the Queen. As a token of appreciation, the captured banner of the enemy was placed in the chapel of Jasna Gora. They also promised to visit the Blessed Mother, there at the shrine, every year as a sign of thanksgiving for this victory.

They kept this promise for almost 137 years when, in 1754, they forgot about it. God, however, soon reminded them. Behold, an unexpected hail storm destroyed all their crops that year. This warning was a new stimulus to continue the fulfillment of a promise once made.

THE CAVE-IN

The miners were busy as usual one day in 1609. They were digging deep down in the dimly lit bowels of the earth, mining lead and silver ore. Five husky men were working in one of the deepest shafts. They were Jakob Gola, Walenty Lomigonek, Jakob Piwoworek, Simon Budzinkowiec and his brother, John.

EXPLOSION

They went about their work in routine fashion when, all of a sudden, a terrific explosion shook the supported walls around them and they found themselves partially covered by falling sand and timbers.

After freeing themselves they tried to escape, but soon learned that every avenue of escape was closed and completely sealed by the falling debris. It did not take long for them to realize that they were buried in a tomb, some ninety feet below the surface.

NO APPARENT HOPE OF ESCAPE

Terrible, indeed, was their plight and they soon appreciated the gravity of their position, being completely shut off from the living world with no hope of escape. Even if help did come, they knew from the previous experience of others, that it could not possibly arrive in time. No one could be so naive as to even hope to exist without food, light and air so deep in the ground, until a new shaft could be excavated.

FAITH AND NEW HOPE

Despite the apparent hopelessness of their plight, the brave and pious mountaineers did not despair. They did not lose hope of freedom and liberation. They firmly believed that God would not forsake them. So they all fell on their knees and pledged a solemn promise to Our Lady of Czestochowa, that when liberated from this terrible tomb and death, they would make a special pilgrimage to Jasna Gora. They continuously pleaded and begged for help and deliverance.

ON THE SURFACE

Above, on the surface of the mine, the scene was even more heartbreaking. The families of the unfortunate victims, after being informed of the terrible catastrophe, hurried to the scene of the cave-in. The wives, mothers, and children of the trapped miners frantically tried to dig into the covered pit. Only with difficulty could they be kept away. Finally, they realized that all human efforts were in vain. It was then that they turned to fervent prayer, begging and pleading with Our Madonna of Czestochowa to help their trapped fathers, husbands and sons.

EXCAVATION BEGINS

In the meantime, every available mountaineer from the entire vicinity responded to the emergency call. They applied themselves with every ounce of energy at their disposal, digging without a moment's rest to free the trapped comrades. For many days, they continued digging until their strength began to give way and they found themselves on the verge of collapse from exhaustion; but they all continued to pray.

The nights, with their depressing darkness, added to the gloom and apparent hopelessness of the situation. Everyone present knew only too well, that the longer it took them to dig out the collapsed shaft the less chance of survival remained for the men below.

Despite every difficulty and temporary set-back, both on top as well as under the ground, suppliant and fervent prayer continued. They were all strengthened by a firm faith in the power of the Blessed Mother, believing that she would never disappoint those who had recourse to her. The entire five days of waiting and brutal hard work seemed like an eternity.

RESCUE

On the fifth day, the entombed men heard a faint echo of pounding picks. Their faith was reaffirmed that, finally, the Madonna of Czestochowa was sending help and the more fervent became their prayer. After another lapse of time, which seemed like an age, they felt refreshed by a sudden gust of fresh air. Looking up they saw a flicker of light from the approaching miners' lamps in the distance, as the opening in the wall of their tomb began to widen.

Indescribable was the surprise and astonishment of the diggers when, instead of corpses, they found the five imprisoned men in perfect health.

THANKSGIVING

Soon, however, their astonishment and surprise changed to thanksgiving. They learned from the liberated men that they attributed their salvation to the intercessory power of Our Lady of Jasna Gora. There was no end thereafter to the chant of admiration and thanksgiving by the families of the rescued men. The next day, all the miners, their families and the entire countryside made a special pilgrimage to Jasna Gora to personally thank the Madonna.

This miracle inspired an artist to paint the beautiful fresco on the ceiling of the main chapel on Jasna Gora.

THE AMBASSADOR

Stefan Osowski, from the house of Gryf, province of Lubelski, was sent as special ambassador from Poland to the Court of the Sultan of Turkey. He received his commission and orders in 1628. Accompanied by Pan Ozga, a captain from Trembowli, he set out on the journey to the metropolitan city and soon completed his mission.

EXCURSION

With plenty of time at his disposal before returning to Poland, Mr. Osowski decided to take a cruise to the Asian mainland. A choice group of selected friends accompanied him on this excursion. At first, the pleasure of the trip surpassed all expectations as they glided along in ideal weather on a quiet sea.

THE STORM

Suddenly, the smiling sky became overcast with dark, threatening clouds. A sharp wind whipped up and began to blow the ship in a reckless frenzy. Rain came down in torrents. The waves grew to mountainous proportions and the frail craft creaked and groaned as it was tossed about. One moment it seemed it was lost in the deep ravines between the waves; then the teeth of the whirling gale were trying to chew it into splinters.

In mortal fear and on the verge of despair, the spirit of the passengers was dampened still more as they saw the crew members, one by one, become helpless due to overexertion.

PRAYER

Making his final preparation for death, Ambassador Osowski, in his meditation, suddenly recalled that, suspended from his neck on his breast, he had a medal of the Madonna of Czestochowa. It was a matter of fact that the Polish knight never left the boundaries of Poland without his medal.

Osowski took this sacred emblem and hung it on the wall of the cabin and with all the passengers, lay down, prostrate on the slippery watersoaked deck before this image. In confidence, he entrusted himself and the entire entourage to the care of the Blessed Lady, with a promise of special respects to the Madonna of Jasna Gora.

SALVATION

Their prayer was heard in Heaven. Suddenly, Mary, the mother of the One to whom all elements are obedient, stretched out her helping hand. As if taken away by an invisible touch, the winds subsided; dark clouds dispersed and the waves quieted down so that the journey was finished in peace just as it started.

THANKSGIVING

Grateful, all survivors visited Czestochowa soon after arrival in Poland.

A TRUE SOLDIER

It was during the epidemic of 1743, one of the many which frequently plagued early Poland, that Colonel Stanislaw Jazowski was traveling through the stricken area and there decided to put up for the night. Suddenly, he felt sick and noticed his temperature rising steadily. It did not take a lengthy diagnosis before he became convinced that he, too, was a victim of the plague. Living up to the tradition of a true soldier, he refused to submit and although feeling extremely tired and weak, he drove off. His journey was of a very short duration for he soon fell off the horse, unconscious.

ACCIDENT

As complete darkness enveloped the countryside, he lay there exposed to the elements, on a rarely traversed road, more so now during the epidemic. The people left their homes and fled into the forests, there seeking protection by avoiding contact with other germ-carrying individuals. Regaining his senses, the colonel tried to rise but was too weak and exhausted. He felt himself growing weaker, tormented by terrible thirst and mounting fever which were gradually burning his throat and body.

He lay there like Lazarus of the Gospel, raising his tired eyes to Heaven, as death approached and painful convulsions seized his emaciated body. He did not care to die because he wanted to stay in the service of his fatherland and help the family to greater attainments here on earth.

THE PRAYER

Being too weak to utter a word, he raised his heart to God in sincere prayer and begged, "Our Lady of Czestochowa, help me." At that moment, he lost consciousness and fell into a deep sleep. In the sleep that followed, he saw himself lying on the ground and above, in the clouds, a bright figure illumined by golden rays from the sun. This vision he recognized as the Blessed Virgin Mary. His heart began to beat very rapidly and was filled with some supernatural joy and love so that he could not utter a word.

The brilliance of the figure blinded him as he tried to rise but could not move. Then, the Blessed Virgin, with all the tenderness of a true mother, came to him and placing her hand on his head whispered, in a heavenly sweet voice — "Fear not, you will live."

He sprung up as the vision disappeared, well and healthy again as ever before. He found his horse nearby and continued the interrupted journey, ever grateful to the Madonna of Jasna Gora.

MADONNA APPEARS TO A FUTURE MONK

This happened in 1552. Ensign Mikolaj Boglewski, a great friend of a certain Stefan Wodynski, was tendered a very sumptuous reception and party. As was customary in the old Polish homesteads of the wealthy, the wine and food were of the best. The environment, coupled with congenial friends, helped to instill a certain spirit of joy and happiness into the gay moods of all present, which no words could appraise properly.

It was rather early morning when the ensign and his entourage started for home. Being a good rider, once he mounted the Arabian pony, he let loose the reins and disappeared in the darkness of the dawn ahead of his friends. The road to his estate led through a dark and dense forest. Suddenly, his horse came upon a tree which was felled across the path and while trying to leap over it, threw the rider; stumbling, he fell on the ensign crushing him with his weight.

When the jubilant servants arrived at the scene of the accident, their mood changed to terror as they freed their master from under the horse. They found that his heart had stopped beating and the ensign's body was already in the grip of death.

In near despair and overcome by fright, they all fell to the ground prostrate and began to call on Our Lady of Czestochowa for help, with a promise to be ever grateful to her.

VISION

In the meantime, the ensign, as he later attested, lay there senseless and unconscious of what was actually happening around him but was tortured by a weird vision. Indescribable apparitions began to ridicule and torture him immensely. The terrified servants saw how he twitched and turned as if in great pain. His body began to quiver and it seemed that it wanted to shake free the very soul within. Then, the vision changed. The Madonna of Czestochowa stood before him and, embracing him, with one sweep of her cloak drove the evil spirits away. This instilled new confidence and courage in his heart. After the vision disappeared, the ensign rose to his feet and continued his journey homeward without any ill effects. Soon after, he made a special visit to Jasna Gora where he thanked the Blessed Mother for the miraculous rescue from death.

Later, he entered the Pauline Fathers and was instrumental in building the new cloister.

THE PRINCESS

Princess Anna Wisniowiecka was very active among the younger set of the upper class and especially interested in the outdoor sportsman's life. One beautiful summer day in 1613, she decided to go boat riding on a quiet but deep river in the neighborhood of her parents' palatial estate. The day was ideal, so she simply floated down with the current and, in a pensive mood, enjoyed the passing scenery, reminiscing about the glorious days of her early youth.

THE STORM

Suddenly, the world seemed to turn upside down. A strong wind whipped up from nowhere; the clouds turned from serene blue to ugly black and the quiet flowing river became an angry maelstrom.

To make matters worse, the princess became so frightened when she was rudely awakened from her pensive mood, that all courage left her. In her fright, she lost the oars and failing to hold on to the rocking boat, was tossed into the churning waves of the angry river. The mistress stood on the shore, helpless, since she did not know how to swim and there was no adequate help in sight.

PLEA

Then, above the howling of the storm and the splashing water, the suppliant voice of the princess could be heard — "Our Lady of Czestochowa, help me." It was to her protectress that Anna turned in this moment of distress because she always trusted her. Our Blessed Mother heard the voice of the princess and answered the call.

ANSWER

Just as Peter was saved by the Master on the Sea of Galilee, the Blessed Mother of Czestochowa appeared to the princess, dressed in a beautiful cloak bedecked with priceless jewels and, with a smile, took the young lady by the hand and led her safely to shore over the raging water.

Later, the princess presented a silver plaque in Czestochowa commemorating her rescue.

A DEAD INFANT

In the presence of helpless and grief-stricken parents, Antoni and Anna Karwat, who lived in Salicia, their little daughter, Jozefa Magdalena, but a few months old, suddenly became ill and died in 1747. The unfortunate mother threw herself on the little corpse of her daughter, trying as it were to protect the infant from the enveloping power of merciless death. Despite all earthly efforts, death proved to be much more powerful, for it is a known fact, that once it takes a person in its cold, bony fingers, no created power can save him from complete submission. All night she actually bathed the little lifeless body of the infant in her tears while begging Mary of Czestochowa to return to her the little deceased daughter.

The friends and relatives began to scold her, saying, "You expect the Blessed Mother to resurrect your child — you are not worthy of it; stop your lamenting and give to the earth that which belongs to it." All of a sudden, the lined face of the suffering mother became illumined by a heavenly light, as if strengthened by some infused vigor and determination. She stood upright and, facing the assembled mourners, said, "You do not understand me. If my child does not come to life here, I am taking her to Czestochowa and there, for sure, the Blessed Mother will restore her life and health." Having said this, she picked up the miniature casket containing the little stiffened corpse and, sitting down in a wagon, began to pray in audible tones; then, with confidence, commenced the painful journey to Jasna Gora.

THE MIRACLE

The Blessed Mother, however, did not wait for them to arrive at her shrine. She decided to reward the lively faith of the mother in her intercessory power and immediately restored the soul to the dead body of the little girl. At the moment when the little child showed signs of life, all those present fell on their knees and, as if in one voice, they cried, — "A miracle! A miracle! Oh, how powerful you are, Mary of Jasna Gora!"

The happy mother continued her journey to Czestochowa but in her loving arms she now held little Jozefa Magdalena, smiling and very much alive instead of the lifeless little corpse overpowered by death. They arrived at Jasna Gora and offered their thanks.

BELIEVING MOTHER

It seemed that Malgorzata Zloczewska would cry her eyes out when her son, Stefan, became seriously ill in 1674. Despite all setbacks however, the grieving mother made a solemn vow to Our Lady of Czestochowa, that if she would restore her son's health, in return she would buy and donate a gold memento to the shrine. The mother was truly broken-hearted as she watched her beloved son in pain, slowly failing. Finally, death was victorious as Stefan passed away in the arms of his distraught mother. Although it seemed at the moment that the Blessed Mother refused to listen to Malgorzata because, despite her prayers and vows, the son was dead, she did not lose confidence in the intercessory power of the Madonna of Jasna Gora. She paid no attention to the fact that

Stefan's soul had left his body and returned to its Maker; she continued to believe ever more firmly that the Queen of Jasna Gora would bring him back. She was convinced that for the Virgin Mary, God will grant any favor. The bereaved mother understood this whole transition as a test of her faith, convinced that the only reason why God took her son's soul was simply to return it again.

PRAYER

Malgorzata Zloczewska continued to pray. In near ecstasy, she renounced all attachment to this world's blessings and enveloped, as it were, her heart and soul in confidential and persevering prayer. Placing herself in the presence of God in contemplation, suddenly as though in a dream, she heard the excited voice of the nurse watching over the little corpse, that his eyes were moving; that the lifeless body was regaining its natural color and qualities.

The mother, as if inspired by some supernatural impulse, rushed into the room with a joyous outcry, "Stefan is alive." And true it was; Our Lady of Czestochowa returned the son who had been dead to the waiting arms of a happy and thankful mother.

MIRROR OF JUSTICE

During the occupation of Poland in 1715 by the Swedish armies, one of the invaders was secretly murdered in cold blood. After routine investigation, suspicion rested on a certain Michal Lagowski, a painter, but the fact was, that this man was completely innocent.

After being apprehended and judged by an improvised military court, Michal was found guilty and sentenced to die by hanging. On the eve of the execution day assigned by the court, as the condemned prisoner sat alone in a dark dungeon, bound in heavy chains, he sadly reflected over his unfortunate lot. He did not despair however, but accepting this situation as a fulfillment of God's will, he persevered in prayer. Michal Lagowski was a devout and practicing believer in God.

APPARITION

Sitting there enveloped in complete darkness, suddenly he was startled by a flash of light which streaked across one side of the room; shortly afterwards the entire underground prison dungeon became bright as if illumined by a bright noon day sun. There, before him in full view, Michal saw the Madonna of Czestochowa with the Infant Jesus in her arms, beaming with a supernatural brightness, who said to him, "Son! Because you have never neglected devotions to me and on Saturdays you fasted in my honor, I now come to your rescue; rise and go to Czestochowa; no one will stand in your way." After this, the Madonna disappeared.

FREEDOM

What a surprise when the prisoner stood up and saw the chains binding him, fall to the ground! There were six Swedish soldiers standing guard over him, and they were petrified by the vision when they saw and heard the Madonna. They unlocked the prison doors and with great reverence asked the prisoner to go free.

Thus it happened just as the Blessed Mother told him. Unharmed and unmolested, he went to Czestochowa to express his gratitude for the miraculous liberation.

THE MONK'S ADVICE

A malady of the eyes harassed James Poznanski of Grabowca. He spent his personal fortune to purchase medicine but to no avail. The ailment grew worse, finally resulting in blindness. He spent many years in this condition.

On a certain day in 1592, a Capuchin priest came to the town and visited James. The monk was amazed at the suffering and began to console the afflicted man. In concluding his visit, the monk told Mr. Poznanski about Our Lady of Czestochowa and urged him to beg her for his recovery. No sooner were the words spoken than James decided to follow the advice of the pious monk.

With a firm faith and an unshaken hope in the power of Mary, he began the long journey to Jasna Gora. Our Blessed Mother, always merciful to those afflicted with this dreadful ailment, confirmed James' faith, for in the course of his journey, he felt a slight relief. The nearer he approached to the holy place, the less he seemed to suffer. Acts of faith and hope were renewed; he commended himself to Our Lady of Czestochowa by singing and praying. With each mile his soul rejoiced and the pain in his eyes lessened.

He reached Czestochowa. At the threshold of the chapel a strange sensation enveloped him which he could not describe; he became frightened; he was alarmed and trembling. At one moment he heard nothing, felt nothing; nevertheless, his heart was full of hope that something was about to happen. He entered the miraculous chapel and here the grace of Mary of Jasna Gora descended upon the chosen one. The eyes which were darkened for many years were cured by one glance from Our lady. A miracle took place! James Poznanski saw the sacred portrait of Mary and, with an outcry of joy mingled with love and gratitude, he fell prostrate before Our Lady of Czestochowa in thanksgiving.

THE JUDGE

It is often said that even the bravest and strongest characters are afraid to die, especially at the moment when death is near them.

Back in 1620, when an epidemic spread throughout Poland, there lived a certain Hon. Samuel Kaluski, a judge in Liwia. Seeing that almost half the community's population was already taken by death, he became extremely frightened. To protect himself and his family, he barricaded all exits and entrances of his home and allowed no one to so much as come near his mansion.

ESCAPE

For a while, it seemed that his plan was a success, but in the face of such an epidemic neither doors nor locks and chains can be barriers strong enough to keep death away. One day he discovered that his little daughter had become ill — a victim of the epidemic and her body was covered with sores and blotches from head to foot. Soon, the nursemaid also contracted the same disease and both died in horrible, excruciating pain. This added no little terror to the already mounting fear of the judge.

As a last resort, the judge, driven almost to madness, took his wife, three children and a servant and fled into the woods. It could not be said that they lived but merely existed amid great hardship caused by rain, heat, hunger, and cold. They built a crudely constructed shelter of branches which they gathered from the forests. This was totally inadequate because the wind would scatter their fire and rain would soak the bedding. On cloudy and cold nights, they huddled together near the fire and stared into the dark night. Even the slightest noise or movement in the dark forest would fill them with fear. The mother would embrace the scared little children; the father, himself uneasy, would try to pacify them while the faithful servant would try to console them.

VICTIM

One day, Mr. Kaluski himself felt the chills, followed by fever and general weakness. Then, the dreaded sores appeared over his entire body. He was the first victim of the dread disease here in the isolated forest. Death was inevitable under existing circumstances.

PRAYER

Not giving up, this is what the judge did. With all his strength and great humility of a believing heart, Judge Samuel Kaluski consecrated himself, his family and all the servants at the mansion to the Blessed Mother with a promise, that if the family was spared by God, they would all make a special pilgrimage on foot to the shrine of Czestochowa.

ANSWER

The Blessed Mother accepted this promise and answered the fervent prayer. The judge rose from the sick bed and, to the great surprise of the overjoyed family, his body was cleansed of every sore. They returned to their family home, grateful to the Madonna of Jasna Gora.

It was revealed later, that from the day on which Mr. Kaluski made his solemn consecration, not one person in the village became sick or died from the disease.

Grateful to the Blessed Mother for this miracle, the judge and his family visited the shrine on Jasna Gora on August 15, the Feast of the Assumption. Here, he dedicated a plaque in the name of his entire family with this inscription, "To the Heavenly Protectress from all deadly disease."

LIBERATION

On the palatial estate of one of the well-known Polish families (the name is not given for obvious reasons), the jovial master and his entire family led a very merry and somewhat lavish existence. The moving force behind the very life of this family was young and beautiful Anna, the daughter of the master, whose vivacious disposition and fun-loving attitude added a great deal to the pleasure of living in the age-old palatial walls of the mansion. Some of the most distinguished people of the era frequently met here at banquets, dances and friendly socials. It seemed to all those who knew the family that the rays of the bright sun would never set on the happy environment.

MISFORTUNE

Suddenly, like a thunderbolt from the clear sky, misfortune disturbed this peaceful and happy household. What made it so much more difficult to take and bear was the fact that the catastrophe concentrated its full destructive force on the beloved daughter, Anna.

This is what happened. The young lady, irritated by one of her girl attendants, flew into a violent rage and, forgetting herself momentarily, inadvertently uttered some blasphemous word. In that very moment, the evil spirit took possession of her entire being. From this day on, hours of gloom, depression and pitiful sorrow began in the palace. The events which followed were more than weird.

Instead of the joyous music which resounded with such melody in the halls of the palace, frightful and hair-raising screams were heard from Anna who was now tortured by the devil; instead of the usual hilarious and approving laughter, sobbing of the unhappy parents depressed everyone; instead of lively dances, the devil would manipulate the body of the helpless victim, at times throwing it to the ground, then again beating it with unimaginable cruelty. Even the neighbors and relatives had to move away from the neighborhood, as if it were contaminated. All the roads leading to the estate, once well kept, now became almost impassable, overgrown with wild weeds and grass. The servants and other attendants, greatly disturbed by the inhuman howling of the possessed, contemplated escape. This horrible condition last twelve months. During this time, the helpless parents continuously called priests who preformed exorcisms as prescribed by the Church; innumerable and fervent prayers were said; every imaginable form of alms was given, but all this organized effort seemed to have been wasted since no results could be seen.

PILGRIMAGE

The parents did not give up. To them the only solution to the problem was Jasna Gora where they firmly believed help could be obtained. So, in 1632, they brought Anna to the very modest earthly abode of the Blessed Madonna. Here, spending their time in prayer and reinforced by a firm faith in the power of the Blessed Virgin, they remained with Anna for three weeks. During this entire time, the girl behaved so normally that everyone believed her to be finally liberated. It was then decided to return home in the company of two priests.

On their way, the party stopped at Klobucek and it was here that the torments returned. The devil was dormant for a short while so that he could intensify his fury. Awakened at night by the hair-raising cries of the possessed, the friars quieted her a little with holy water, and again the disturbed group returned to Jasna Gora. At the moment when the tip of the cloister spire appeared on the horizon to the weary travelers, they instantly fell prostrate on their faces in the middle of the road and, inspired by deep faith, they begged the Madonna for a miracle.

Suddenly the devil, holding full possession of the victim, began to roar with such force, through the mouth of the young lady, that all were overcome with great fear, but did not stop praying. Then, the devil, for the last time, threw the now distorted body of the victim against the ground with such force, that the frail and colorless remains were left almost lifeless. The evil spirit was defeated, never to come back. After a while, Anna was revived and brought to Jasna Gora. She felt as if reborn in body and soul.

THANKSGIVING

The parents, grateful for the miraculous liberation of their daughter, offered the lady of Jasna Gora a gold chalice, set with costly pearls and enriched the chapel by installing a very expensive marble floor.

The young lady completely changed her way of life after this escape. She renounced the beauty and vanity of this world and entered the convent of Saint Clare and offered herself to the service of God. After extolling the goodness and wonders of Czestochowa, she attained a high degree of sanctity and holiness.

"MOTHER, I SEE GOD!"

Mary Ann Gasinska, from Bystrej near Sombar, had a seven year old daughter who was blind for two years. The mother was deeply grieved by this because she foresaw the wretched future of the poor child once she was to be deprived of her maternal care. It was for this reason she performed sacrifices of prayer, fasting and almsgiving, but all seemed in vain because the child did not improve.

In May, 1811, Mary Ann doubled the efforts of her prayers because it was the month of May. One day as she was praying, which was nothing new to the mother, she had a sudden inspiration to take a trip to Czestochowa and visit the Blessed Mother. She knew this to be a place where special privileges were granted to those searching for help and she believed that, here, Mary might answer her prayers sooner. She prepared for the pilgrimage and on May 15, she left with Elizabeth to make the planned visit.

The journey with a blind child became very difficult and troublesome. The child was too big to be carried; yet she was lame and small enough that she could not manage by herself. Despite the hardships, Mrs. Gasinska made every effort to visit each church she passed in order to renew, with greater fervor and more hope, her petition to the Lady of Jasna Gora. On the third day of the journey, i.e., the 18th day of May (they traveled only 5 miles) she stopped with the child in the town of Tuchow to hear Mass as she was accustomed to do. She fell prostrate in front of a cross before the altar while the Holy Sacrifice was being offered and, overcome with tears, she pleaded with Our Lady of Czestochowa for the child. Elizabeth, the daughter, knelt beside her mother with hands folded, united in prayer which her beloved mother had taught her. In a moment Mary Ann sensed that the child had become restless as she raised her head and noticed that the child's face no longer had the expression of a blind person. Then the child seemed to be amazed as her eyes began to take in the view of the altar and people. At once the child turned to her mother and whispered, "Mother, I see God, you and everyone!" At these words an indescribable joy stirred the depressed heart of the mother. She took the child, pressed her to her bosom and, in words of appreciation, thanked the Madonna. She continued her journey to Jasna Gora to offer further thanksgiving to Our Lady of Czestochowa.

IMPRISONED, EXILED, AND PERSECUTED

After the partition of Poland by her enemies, the republic rebelled with the hope of overthrowing the yoke of captivity. Twice, in 1830 and in 1838, the youth of Poland organized an uprising, in defense of faith and freedom, only to meet bitter defeat. The results of their endeavors were: filled prison cells and great anguish. The citadel cisterns flowed with martyrs' blood; the country became a forest of gallows; men and women were sent to Siberia or were massacred by the Cossacks. In schools, the use of the mother tongue was forbidden and persecution was ordered to punish the firmly believing men and women. The spirit of the nation was weakened by the enemy. In fact, it would have been shattered entirely if not for the help from Jasna Gora. Just as the thirsty seek drink, so did the faithful of the three divided portions of Poland speed to Mary for comfort. It was here that their spirit was strengthened, their hope stimulated and their desire to fight rekindled.

CZESTOCHOWA, THE CENTER

At this time neither Warsaw, nor Cracow, nor Poznan were the centers of Poland, but Jasna Gora where Mary the Queen of the Nation and of Poland ruled. After many years of oppression nothing could unite a nation thus partitioned and governed by three masters; yet this unity was found at Jasna Gora. Here at the feet of Mary, the faithful expressed the same sentiments and the same expressions of love. Who healed the wounded hearts of hundreds of prisoners who were seeking freedom? Whose name and whose aid was summoned by the lips of everyone? It was the sweet name of Mary! Recourse was made to her because she gave aid and comfort; the very thought of Mary reconciled the people to the will of God. What became of the unfortunate and forsaken prisoners in Siberia? What was the reaction of those who were chained and forced to slave labor in the coal mines? Was there any despair or loss of faith? No! — a hundred times no! — during the many wintry nights, the minds of the people were illuminated, as it were, with memorable sights of Jasna Gora. The sweet figure of Our Lady of Czestochowa was a spiritual tonic to those condemned to the coal mines. On the coarse and gloomy subterranean walls the vision of Our Lady of Czestochowa with the Child was seen by all amid rays brighter than the sun. The faithful knelt and with outstretched blood-stained hands, prayed in a firm voice, "Hail Queen, Oh Blessed Mother!" After each of these visions, they were comforted in spirit, their fears quieted, their wounds healed as if by a soothing balm. For that reason they accepted suffering voluntarily and offered it to God for the satisfaction of the sins of the nation, with a petition for liberation.

One of these heavenly visions was painted by a famous Polish artist, Arthur Grottger.

Thus it was that Mary unified a torn nation, appeased their sorrow, and lessened their troubles; from Jasna Gora she increased the nation's courage and strengthened the faith so symbolic of the Polish people.

In 1875, the Russians persecuted the people in the manner of Nero and Diocletian. The land was crimsoned again with the blood of martyrs. The accused were sent to prison or to Siberia — all in the hope of eradicating their strong faith. But once again Jasna Gora became a focal point. The memory of the towers brought comfort and consolation. They recalled to the oppressed people that Mary, the Mother of God, reigns from her throne in Czestochowa. This, in itself, was an inspiration to the people to hold firm to their faith, even at the expense of suffering and death. In the darkness of night, the faithful came to the Blessed Mother to receive her blessings and beg for the Sacraments. These were the people who carried blessed medals, catechisms and inspirational hope to the other poor victims. In the name of Mary, the people fought and died for their faith and sought hope in Mary's protection to regain freedom.

On the vaults of the Basilica of Jasna Gora are seen paintings depicting the release of captives. These miracles are recorded in the register of Jasna Gora and they number 59.

THE CONVERT

The Queen of Czestochowa granted special graces and help not only to the Polish people but also to all those who, with faith and confidence, had recourse to her.

AN ENGLISH SUBJECT

A subject of the crown of England, Sebastian by name, arrived at the port of Gdansk in 1589. While sojourning there, he was enlightened by the special grace of God so that he changed his religious conviction. Overnight, from a perverted heretic, he became a devout Catholic. This, of course, greatly incensed his brother who used every possible means at his disposal, some even quite dishonorable, to stop Sebastian from embracing Catholicism.

BACK TO ENGLAND

After a brief stay in Poland, Sebastian and his irate brother started the journey homeward to their native England. Their progress across the Baltic was suddenly impeded by a terrific storm.

PERSECUTION

As the general situation became more acute and hopeless, it seemed that all would be swallowed by the enraged sea. The older brother took advantage of the situation. He again began to use pressure on Sebastian to renounce his newly accepted Catholic faith and return to the old Calvinist conviction. His words however, did not produce the desired effect, so he took recourse to violence.

After having Sebastian bound with ropes, he ordered him to be thrown into the turbulent sea on the end of a rope and dragged at the side of the boat. Again he insisted that Sebastian renounce his new faith. The young man, however, remained firm in his new conviction.

Finally, enraged to a point of madness by the firmness and determination of Sebastian, he cut him adrift in the raging sea. Like a helpless feather in the wind, the victim was cast about by the foaming waves. Suddenly, a mountainous wave raised him high above the rough sea; terrified, his gaze searched for a sign of others but no one was in sight. Even the ship with his brother had disappeared beyond the swelling horizon.

RESCUE

Even at this dire moment Sebastian did not despair. He recalled the devout attachment of the Polish people as well as their belief and trust in the Blessed Mother, whom they lovingly call the Madonna of Czestochowa. He went to Jasna Gora in spirit, as he raised his heart in prayer prompted by a firm faith. He turned to the Blessed Mother with a pitiful cry, but full of confidence — "Save me lest I perish."

Suddenly, from nowhere a strange ship appeared at his side and the surprised crew spotted the floating victim tossed about in the water. Soon ropes and life boats were lowered and Sebastian was pulled aboard.

THANKSGIVING

One year later, grateful Sebastian now a more fervent Catholic than ever, returned from distant England to Poland. At the shrine of the Madonna of Czestochowa, he offered his prayer of thanksgiving.

UNBELIEVER

This is the testimony of Anna Korsak, from Lublin, who was miraculously cured on May 29, 1921.

"I would like to describe in detail what happened to me on this memorable day of May 29. In the beginning of 1919, I was afflicted with a critical malady of the eyes. It consisted of the inflammation of the retina together with a terrible disturbance of the entire eye. The overall ailment tired me terribly. I knew physiology well enough to foresee the outcome: blindness was inevitable. The help of famous eye doctors and specialists was sought. In fact, I was under treatment by the famous eye specialist, Doctor Naiszauski, a professor at the University of Petersgrad, and yet my eyesight was getting worse all the time. In February and March of 1921, with the help of strong eyeglasses, I could not even distinguish letters; reading had become impossible for me. The headaches which I had, became more severe. It seemed that my brain was being drawn out of my skull and my eyes felt as if lashed by a whip. These headaches occurred more often and became more intense. In fact the only relief I could have was by sitting in darkness and using various radical treatments for my head. At a distance of two steps I could not distinguish people, many a time speaking to my father I mistook him for my mother. The only way I could distinguish people was by their voices. This was a veritable martyrdom for me.

PILGRIMAGE

Before this I was a confirmed unbeliever. Nevertheless, I had some kind of craving for security and for aid from the church. Then, like a ray of light, a thought stirred in my mind about Czestochowa! On May 29, 1921 I arrived at the famous chapel. Deep emotion overcame me and I again reassured myself that nowhere else on this earth could I receive help and that this was the only place for the cure of my ailment. Before this portrait many cures had already taken place.

I stood for a moment — Did I pray? Yes, but in what manner? I cannot say. What were my thoughts, what words did I use? I do not know. I am sure of this, I did not see nor did I hear anything. Without a doubt I prayed as best I could. How long? I do not know.

In a moment I was aware of what I was doing; I felt a light blinding me and thousands of flicking flames all around me. Mingled in the crowd, I heard the woman beside me praying. I asked her, 'Where is the Miraculous Portrait?' 'Here it is,' came the answer, 'here is the famous chapel.' 'Yes,' I answered, 'but show me the place where the picture is because I do not see it.' 'Over there, where the candles are lit, above them is the head of the Blessed Lady.' Around me I heard: 'It is a blind person.' I fell upon my knees — 'Blind person! Dear Lord! — Mercy. O Blessed Lady, have mercy on me.'

THE CURE

My heart was beating rapidly and I was sobbing. As the brightness of the lights struck my eyes, I became aware of all the sins of my life; what deep sorrow overcame me, whereby I was moved to contrition and tears. 'Tears, — that is death to your eyes' were the words of doctors — 'Avoid emotion.' But everything is the same; I prayed, I begged and I cried. To see her, if only for a moment, and then let God do what he wishes, even if it is blindness forever.

I raised by eyes; all I saw was a dark spot instead of the Portrait. An unexplainable pain moved my soul, and from the bottom of my heart I sent a petition to Mary. I prayed with renewed vigor: 'I will change my life, I will give up everything, avoid pleasures, fashions, most of all I will be pure; I did not attend church, now I crave to receive Holy communion everyday.'

Again I raised my eyes. O, Lord! What is this? A crown on the child's head. 'I can see!' was my joyous outcry. My eyes were glued to the portrait; the vision of fire left me and all I could see was the sweetest face of Our Lady of Jasna Gora. Almost unconscious from happiness, I approached the altar on my knees and all the possessions I had — remembrances, jewelry, money, I gave as an offering. Overwhelmed with joy, I ran to the Sisters' home where my sister was staying and awaiting me. I asked for a newspaper and glancing with ease I read and shouted, 'I am reading; I am reading! Oh, what joy.' After this, I was blessed with a serene peace.

From then on I could read and learn. I entered the Catholic University of Lublin and majored in History. I am, at present, finishing my examinations with success. I have already passed Logic, Psychology, Polish History, German History and Encyclopedia. The only examination yet to be taken is Latin. I can hardly believe my success whereby, instead of being blind and unhappy until death, I am of service to myself and to others in the field of education.

Every step, every task begins with God. Every year on the 29th of May, I visit 'Jasna Gora' and there spend a day of retreat offering my soul and my heart at the feet of the Heavenly Mother and Doctor."

(This letter is a part of the Monastery archives.)

THE MUTE

In 1597, a pilgrimage to Jasna Gora started from Kamilnica. The journey was to begin when a certain Martin Obietynski approached the leaders. He was blind, deaf and dumb from youth. With great effort he was able to explain his desire to go to Czestochowa to beg for a favor and a cure. Moved by his pitiable condition and firm faith, the understanding pilgrims accepted him into their company and saw to it that he was well taken care of during the entire journey. The journey lasted a few weeks, and during this time, Martin behaved like a saint.

Finally, the group, fatigued, yet happy, arrived at Jasna Gora. When the deaf mute was brought to the chapel, he fell prostrate on the floor. Even though he was not able to speak, he actually moaned a prayer to the Blessed Mother. All present understood his inner suffering and gathering around him, joined in prayer for his intention. During the Benediction of the Blessed Sacrament, Martin, as he explained later, felt a power overtaking him and suddenly he arose and loudly proclaimed: "Praised be Jesus Christ and His Mother, Mary." He was cured. This brought great joy to all present.

Martin Obietynski returned home without help.

HOPELESS CASE

At times children in a playful mood become somewhat careless. In 1645, twelve-year old Urszulka, the only child of Marion and Zofja Zalewski, was playing with a pin and while holding it in her mouth, swallowed it.

Hearing the cries of the little girl, the shocked parents and servants investigated. After great difficulty, they learned of the accident from the frightened child. Using all means at their disposal, they tried to help the little girl. Then the doctor was called and even he could not dislodge the pin which stuck in the throat of Urszulka.

The parents could not watch the agony of the child but they did not despair. While the doctor tried to help their child, they prayed in an adjacent room, raising tearful eyes to the Madonna of Czestochowa.

As they prayed more fervently than ever, a strange light illuminated the entire room and on the rays of the bright light, Our Lady of Czestochowa appeared, addressing the disconsolate parents. She said, "Do not weep; your prayers have been heard; your child will be well."

HELP ARRIVES

Not relying on their ears for what they actually heard, nor their eyes for what they had seen, but still full of confidence in the power of Our Lady, they rushed into the sick room to the side of their daughter. They found her in near convulsion brought about by a severe cough. After a while, they noticed that Urszulka spat out the bent and bloody pin which was lodged in her throat.

Soon the entire family joined in grateful prayer at the feet of the Madonna.

REFUGE OF SINNERS

Poverty reigned in the household of the peasant, Bartlomiej and his wife Jadwiga, who lived in the village of Tarczynie. they decided to send their daughter, Anna, to work in the capital city of Warsaw so that her earnings would help defray expenses. After much deliberation and weeping, Anna finally bade farewell to her parents and headed into an unknown but troublesome future.

THE CRIME

Having a good Christian upbringing, Anna was a faithful servant. She led an exemplary life in the employ of some well-to-do people. She was happy in her new role. Unfortunately, after a while, she became acquainted with a man who made many false promises coupled with improper advances which finally led her into serious trouble and disgrace. She gave birth to a child out of wedlock. Ashamed of the evident and living proof of her transgression, and in a moment of utter despair brought about by fear and shame, she threw the helpless infant out the window onto the bank of a nearby river. The very next day, however, the crime was discovered and the guilty party was apprehended by the authorities.

TRIAL

A lengthy trial was held in 1625 and Anna was found guilty by the court and sentenced to die by drowning. While at the prison preparing for the final moment she had ample time to reflect. She recalled her early days of innocence spent happily at the family home. She remembered that poor and simple home in all its peculiar splendor. That remorse led to sorrow and anguish for the home, the village and old folks, upon whom she had brought such disgrace. She wept bitterly, as she envisioned the fact that never again would she be able to see those golden fields of wheat nor take part in the harvest; nor visit the village church in which she was baptized and received her first Holy Communion. Her heart was seized with such great sorrow for the sins committed, coupled with the wounding of God's heart and the saddening of His Most Blessed Mother, that she buried her face in the sod of the bare floor and bathed it in her own tears.

The judges sent the chaplain to the condemned victim, to prepare her for death according to the custom of Holy Mother the Church. Seeing her sincere sorrow for offending Almighty God, the chaplain recommended that Anna turn for help to the Refuge of Sinners — and place herself under the protective care of Our Lady of Czestochowa.

SENTENCE

On the day appointed by the authorities, Anna, accompanied by the prison attendants, was led to the bank of the river. As expected, an inquisitive crowd followed the pitiful procession, curious to see what was to happen. Here the executioner tied a huge stone to her legs to make certain that she would be completely submerged.

There she stood — a young woman in the prime of her youth, full of vigor and eager to live, now on the verge of destruction due to one fatal mistake; one single forgetful moment. Weeping bitter tears, she fell on her knees and before the assembled crowd publicly announced her sorrow for the crime committed and begged God for forgiveness. Then she begged Our Lady of Czestochowa for help and consolation in the moment so difficult to bear. She vowed that if her request would be granted, she would reform her life completely.

EXECUTION

Finally, she ended her sincere but suppliant prayer, and the executioner, fulfilling his duty, threw her into the river from the bridge on which they were standing. As the body of the condemned plunged into the water, the shrill outcry of the victim resounded among the crowded villagers as they cringed and shuddered with horror. Again the treacherous bosom of the river closed in as though nothing happened. The crowd stood petrified, staring helplessly at the waves which a moment ago swallowed up a human life but now flowed on and on as peacefully and serenely as ever before.

MIRACLE

The witnesses stood there in silence for about half an hour, as the Vistula river continued her lazy journey towards the sea. Suddenly, a murmur awakened the bystanders; for, behold, in the distance they saw the surface of the river disturbed, as the form of a girl rose from the depths. They watched her swimming towards the shore with great ease and apparent comfort. With a heavy step, she managed to climb ashore and, standing there, she explained to the silent villagers in a loud voice that while resting on the bottom of the muddy river Our Lady of Czestochowa appeared to her. She claimed the Madonna removed the heavy stone attached to her legs and then ordered her to swim to the shore. To her surprise, she obeyed and easily floated upward.

When Anna finished telling her extraordinary story, the judges and all those present, realizing that a miracle had taken place, fell on their knees. A prayer of thanksgiving to the "Refuge of Sinners" rose to Heaven as everyone prayed.

Not long after this, Anna and her grateful mother, accompanied by many of those who witnessed the miracle, visited Jasna Gora. Here they made a solemn deposition and then returned home to lead an exemplary life.

THE MIGHTY VISTULA RIVER

The Queen of Polish waters is the Vistula river. From time immemorial to this day, she occasionally goes on a periodical rampage. She tears through the dikes as though they were made of paper, flooding the countryside, and leaves the lowlands covered with mud and debris. This is exactly what happened in 1668.

During the height of the overflow, two horse-drawn coaches left Opatow crowded with passengers. Jacek Dombski, from Lubraniec, accompanied by his wife, Anna, and two sons, Andrezej and Pawel, decided to cross the swollen river near Zawickow. Finding this rather impossible at the time, he decided to join the other travelers and cross the river by ferry. One coach was drawn onto the platform of the boat, the other waited for the second crossing.

As the crowded craft was just about in the middle of the river, it was caught in the strong current and tossed about furiously. Suddenly, without warning, the guide line attached to the opposite shore snapped and the two chains holding the carriage secure to the deck, gave way. The coach was plunged into the water. Great was the horror and panic on the boat as the passengers realized that the two Dombski youngsters were in the coach. The terrified parents who stayed on shore with the second coach, stood there helpless, as the foaming water of the rushing river seemed to fill the coach through the opened window.

HELP ARRIVES

This is what they did! At the moment when all seemed lost, the parents fell on their knees and fervently begged the Madonna of Czestochowa for help and assistance. All the people lining the banks of the Vistula joined in a prayerful chant.

The Queen of Jasna Gora came to the rescue. It was a miracle! The coach, instead of sinking to the bottom, began to float quietly on the turbulent surface, even though it was of heavy construction. When help finally arrived and the coach was beached, to the surprise of all present, not one drop of water so much as moistened the inside of the opened cab. Joyfully they found the children safe and sound.

The whole family turned back to Jasna Gora to thank the Blessed Virgin for the miraculous protection.

EPIDEMICS

The people of central Europe were frequently afflicted with serious epidemics during the so-called Middle Ages. This was mostly due to the lack of adequate medical care. History notes many of these critical periods in Poland during the years 1622, 1625, 1630, 1677, and 1707. During those trying years many people died. It is noted that many such towns and cities as Krakow, Warsaw, Lwow and others were almost completely depopulated by these epidemics. Usually the dead were left unburied because there was a shortage of capable people to do the grave digging.

Those who were well and alive escaped into the woods and hideouts believing, that there, away from other people, they could escape with their lives, but even there the grim reaper found them. Normally after such an invasion of death in a locality, famine took over because there was a definite lack of farm hands to till the soil.

History notes this strange phenomena however, that even though all the cities and towns around Jasna Gora were afflicted at one time or another, the city of Czestochowa itself was never touched. It stood out like an island in the midst of a turbulent sea or an oasis in the center of a sandy desert, while the adjoining territory was a veritable graveyard.

It is true that the Pauline Fathers took the necessary means and precautions to hold off the dreaded epidemics but the people attributed their well-being to the direct intervention of the Blessed Mother of Jasna Gora. It was a matter of fact and general belief among the populace, that anyone who willfully ignored the Madonna was a victim of the pestilence while others who adored her, even though they became afflicted, soon became well again.

All those who resided at Jasna Gora, the monks, lay people, and soldiers were always spared from all contamination during the different periods of the epidemics. The Blessed Mother protected her shrine and cohabitants from all diseases.

THE RESURRECTION OF SAMUEL WADZIC

Stanislaw Wadzic and his exemplary wife, Anna, lived in the town of Husiatyn in the county of Kamienicki. All the neighbors knew them to be pious and devout. God Almighty, in His goodness, completed their marital bliss by blessing them with their only child, Samuel, who in 1517, was five years old.

Their routine daily family life continued uninterrupted, at times interwoven with moments of priceless joy and peace, which only the grace of God could give to those who constantly live in His providential presence.

CATASTROPHE!

Suddenly, one day, like a flash of lightning from a clear sky, tragedy struck the peaceful and happy homestead. Samuel, their beloved son, became mortally ill. In vain did they spend sleepless nights; useless became the expensive medicine prescribed and unanswered were their suppliant prayers. After three days, which seemed like a nightmare, the child died, his body distorted by excruciating pain.

The angelic bright eyes were now closed forever, and the smiling innocent lips could no longer speak the words of love, which once resounded like heavenly music to the ears of the now disconsolate parents. It was impossible to describe the suffering of the heartbroken father and mother.

THEY DO NOT DESPAIR

Samuel died on Saturday, the day dedicated in a special manner to Our Beloved Lady, the Mother of God. What did the grief-stricken mother do? She turned to Our Lady of Czestochowa, her heart overflowing with confidence and love, trusting in the Blessed Mother's willingness to help, especially those in trouble. Falling on her knees, in tears, she offered the cold little corpse of her beloved son to Our Lady. Then, she made a solemn promise to undertake a pilgrimage to Jasna Gora. Without a moment's hesitation, she prayed — she pleaded — she begged for mercy.

Night was falling and the scene became more and more depressing as the homestead became shrouded by the cloak of complete darkness. That night seemed to the grief-stricken mother the darkest night she had ever experienced in her life.

No — she could not leave, not even for a moment, the prepared casket in which they placed the frustration of all her earthly dreams and expectations. There she stood, sobbing quietly but unshaken in her faith that the Blessed Mother would not forsake her, even though a deathly pallor had already touched the once beaming countenance of the child.

The father, disturbed to the very essence of his soul, silently sobbed but continued to pray. As the bright sun lifted its rays above the eastern horizon and joyfully announced the beginning of another day, the depressed father went to the parish priest to make the necessary funeral arrangements. It was Sunday morning. In the meantime, the mother persevered in her prayer, now more hopeful than ever before.

THE BLESSED MOTHER ANSWERS HER PRAYER

In the meantime, Our Lady of Czestochowa stood by; she listened. She observed the two devoted hearts torn to shreds by sorrow and suffering. She did not forsake them. The Queen of Jasna Gora assembled, as it were, all the tears of the grief-stricken parents into beautiful sparkling pearls which she studded into her crown. All of a sudden, the deathly pallor disappeared from the corpse. Rigor mortis gave way to normal reflex action. The eyes opened, and the lips began to smile as the little boy, with out-stretched arms, arose from the casket.

THANKSGIVING

When the father returned from church, he found the overjoyed mother with the normally healthy son in her arms. The next day, the happy family fulfilled their promise to Our Lady of Czestochowa when they made their pilgrimage to Jasna Gora.

As a token of their appreciation for this special favor, the overjoyed parents presented two candles the size of the resurrected son to be burned before the Miraculous Portrait of the Madonna of Czestochowa.

UNHAPPY HUSBAND

Andrzej Lewandowski from Wiskitek, not far from Warsaw, married a widow, Maryanna Jasinska, aged 34. This widow was possessed by the devil before her marriage. The evil spirit said many horrible and repulsive things through her, all of which left a bad feeling and impression among her acquaintances.

After her marriage to Lewandowski, the devil did not leave her, but changed his way of acting and became mute, though still very treacherous. Before long, the wife, tormented by both jealousy and hatred towards her husband, turned the household into a veritable hell. Every day it was customary for her to fall into a diabolical rage and in this state she would wreck and destroy everything within reaching distance. She could not perform the normal chores of a housewife. Consequently, the burden of home management and upbringing of the two children from the previous marriage, fell on the shoulders of the poor husband. She would undertake nothing constructive. On the contrary, imbued with satanic cleverness, she made matters more difficult.

In spite of almost superhuman effort, financial collapse threatened the family of Andrzej. No matter what he built or endeavored to improve, she somehow managed to destroy immediately.

FIRST ATTEMPT

One day, after much maneuvering, he succeeded in taking Maryanna to Studzienna, where a miraculous portrait of Our Lady is venerated. Here he prayed for a long time entrusting his wife to her motherly care. One of the fathers of St. Philip said prayers of exorcism over the unfortunate woman.

Maryanna then returned home and for a while it seemed that she was cured. She became exceptionally quiet; but then the spirit of darkness returned and brought back all the former tribulations.

AT CZESTOCHOWA

Almost on the verge of total despair and no longer able to withstand the strain of such a life, the frustrated husband turned to Our Lady of Czestochowa for help. Without much ado, he took his wife, and Antos and Zosia, the two children, to Jasna Gora. After arriving at the miraculous shrine, the woman resisted violently and refused to enter; finally, physical force had to be used. Here, the possessed, falling into a terrible rage, tried to escape. Andrzej had to use all his strength to hold the woman on her knees. Then satan, desiring to use his diabolic power, began to twist the arms and limbs of the victim, at the same time, disheveling her hair and bellowing in a weird, inhuman voice.

The pilgrims in attendance became terrified and ran away from her. The bereaved husband, however, held her down more firmly and with all his heart prayed for her liberation, begging and suppliantly beseeching the Queen of Heaven for help. The innocent voices of the two little children joined in prayer with their stepfather.

THE LIBERATION

One of the witnesses to this gruesome tragedy was a certain Father Thomas Sowinski, an Apostolic Confessor. At the request of her husband, he too joined in prayer for the unfortunate woman. A pitched battle followed. Father Sowinski fought the enemy of God with prayer, fasting and liturgical exorcisms. Victory was won when finally, on July 16, 1802, the woman went to confession and the Immaculate Virgin took compassion upon her. It was the Madonna who again crushed the head of the infernal serpent and liberated Maryanna from satanic obsession on the day of her feast. The evil spirit marshalled together all his diabolic hate and with an inhuman howl left the obsessed, leaving her almost dead on the floor.

Maryanna regained consciousness after some time and began to praise God and His Blessed Mother for the miracle performed. She returned home, a normal housewife, and for many years she lead an exemplary life devoted to the care of her husband and pious upbringing of the two children.

BLIND SON

In 1724, Mr. Ossolinski, a treasurer in the King's Court, was greatly troubled. His youngest son, plagued by an eye ailment, lost his eyesight. The efforts of many doctors were in vain. In a state of near despondency the treasurer called on the Holy Doctor. He forgot his sadness and sorrow. Together with his son, he confidently journeyed to Jasna Gora. They entered the chapel and the father and son, after offering a gold tablet, fell on their knees and prayed fervently.

At that moment the chapel was resplendent in candlelight and before the Miraculous Portrait there were a number of burning votive lamps and lighted candles. Here and there one could detect a sob, or a sigh, or a moan, or even a sincere tear caused by emotion from a grateful heart. In this manner, the faithful begged, thanked and praised the Blessed Lady. From the choir could be heard the joyous strains of the Litany to Mary, by the monks praising the Madonna. As the strains of music descended over the prostrate bodies, and the words of the litany resounded through the chapel, at the moment when the faithful came to the words "Healer of the Sick," the boy had a sudden urge to rise. He raised his head and a cry from his lips could be heard above the chanting, "I see! Now, I see!" In the chapel the faithful stood up petrified. Then they came closer to see the miraculous cure.

Who can express in words the happiness of the mother and the rest of the family when the treasurer returned home with a cured son?

THE BABYSITTER

In the vicinity of Kleczur, Ewa Wozniacka, a professional babysitter, took little Janek for a stroll along the bank of a river. This happened in 1749.

TRAGEDY

As she preoccupied herself momentarily with some little distraction, the little boy running along the bank slipped and plunged into the deep water where he was caught in a strong undertow. Hearing the splash, Ewa ran to help the drowning boy, but before long the little tot disappeared beneath the surface of the turbulent water. Ewa, overcome by fear of punishment, ran away.

The river, however, continued her seaward journey, unconcerned that within her dark womb she had just hidden a young, budding life in the spring of its earthly existence.

A short distance away from the scene of the tragedy, a lady passerby witnessed the entire heartbreaking scene. Having great presence of mind, she immediately notified the mother of the dead child.

Breathless and on the verge of nervous prostration, the poor mother of the boy ran to the scene of the catastrophe; she was followed by many others. A search was started for the submerged corpse but each time the drag nets were pulled out for inspection, the corpse was not there.

Untold grief and sorrow had by now penetrated like poisonous venom into the very essence of the disconsolate mother's soul. Even now it seemed that the stubborn tragic water would refuse to give up the victim. For a long time the diving and dragging operations continued until finally the remains were brought to the shore. Sympathetic friends stood by as little Janek, now motionless in the grip of a deathly pallor, was given back to the sorrowful mother. For surely no one could be so devoid of feeling as not to sympathize with her as she stood there holding the icy, water-soaked body of her beloved son.

PRAYER

In her grief, the ever trusting mother turned her thoughts to Our Lady of Czestochowa. She visualized how once, some time ago, Mary held the limp body of her Divine Son after the Crucifixion. She thought of the Immaculate Heart of Mary as it was pierced by the seven swords of sorrow and she began to appreciate the Virgin's understanding and mercy towards mankind. This is what she did: falling down on her knees, she bathed the lifeless body of her child in her own tears and then offered him to the Queen of Jasna Gora.

When, behold! Our Lady of Czestochowa took pity on this mother for she restored her son back to life as little Janek opened his eyes — smiled and cuddled to the breast of his mother.

"RISE FROM YOUR BED AND WALK!"

One of the most beneficial, as well as destructive elements in nature, is water. Without it, man and life in general, whether   animal or vegetative, cannot exist. But it can cause a great deal of woe and destruction when, at times, it goes on an uncontrolled rampage.

THE FLOOD

It was in the springtime of 1639 that the river, Worta, swelled by the spring thaw and rains, overflowed her banks. Everything in the farmland area was completely submerged under her raging water.

The unfortunate inhabitants of the valley tried to salvage their personal belongings amidst cries of fear and despair, as the rampaging waters continued their methodical course of destruction. The devastated area presented a gruesome picture, made more depressing by the tolling church bells announcing the approaching danger, coupled with the merciless bellowing of the cattle and subdued calls for help from drowning people. The merciless torrent carried away parts of homes, cradles with sleeping children, dead livestock, uprooted trees, furniture and household utensils. Here and there could be seen, amidst the floating debris, a human form, exhausted but clinging to some floating object. On the trees still standing were to be seen partly clothed people of all ages, trembling with fear and calling for help with strained voices. Here and there, rescue boats were to be seen but these were too few to cope with the situation. The bells on church steeples kept on tolling sorrowfully, adding to the horror of the approaching night.

OSTROWSKI HOMESTEAD

On the banks of the Worta, not far from the river, stood the quiet homestead of a certain Stanislaw Ostrowski. After a hard day's work Stanislaw slept as only the exhausted can. During the night he was rudely awakened by the sound of the tolling bells and desperate cries of the people. The noise, coupled with the chill of the night, disturbed him. He jumped out of bed and to his great surprise found himself standing in the water. As he looked out the window, he could see nothing in the darkness but an ocean of water surrounding his home.

Keeping his presence of mind, Stanislaw hurriedly launched a small boat which he always kept in the nearby shed for just such an emergency and quickly found himself tossed about by the foaming waves of the wild river. With all the strength at his disposal, he tried to control the boat with oars but, before long, his strength began to fail him. Powerful whirlpools and mountainous waves threatened to swallow him and the little skiff.

APPARITION

In this moment of near destruction Ostrowski did not despair but, with a confident prayer on his lips, turned for help to Our Lady of Czestochowa. Suddenly, the dark sky above the rampaging tide became illumined as though by a very bright sun and there above him, he saw the most beautiful portrait of Our Lady of Jasna Gora. This apparition, with its brightness, filled him with a strange confidence and power so that he immediately regained his strength and, applying this new vigor to the oars, he soon found himself safe from danger.

ANOTHER MIRACLE

Ten years passed into history from this memorable incident. Ostrowski, during that time, lived happily with his family when suddenly he became mortally ill. After careful and pious preparation for death, he patiently waited for the fulfillment of God's providential will.

Suddenly one day, as he lay there resigned to God's care, an old man with a very pleasant expression on his face appeared to him. He stood before him for a while and then, leaning over close to his face, in a quiet, subdued voice said, "Close your eyes, my son, and rest comfortably." Stanislaw obeyed and, as he closed his eyes, he saw before him Our Lady of Czestochowa, resplendent in her regal heavenly beauty. She came close to him and, taking his hand, said, "Rise from your bed and walk."

In an instant Ostrowski opened his eyes and the apparition disappeared. After describing this celestial scene to his family, he was advised to make a promise to the Blessed Mother, that if restored to good health he would visit her shrine. This he did and as God willed it, he was cured immediately.

MIRACLE AT MASS

In the year 1754, a friar of the Franciscan Order in Pyzdra, a Father Bonaventure Sikarski, was afflicted with an ailment of the eyes and as a result was totally blind for six weeks. The famous priest was depressed and unhappy, yet never lost confidence in the power of Mary, that is why he began a novena to Our Lady of Czestochowa. Strengthened by a deep and fervent faith, he prayed for eight days. On the ninth day, Mary showed her love by moving the edge of the dressing that covered his eyes and Father Bonaventure was able to see a little. Later he made a trip to Jasna Gora so that he could personally plead at the throne of Mary for a total cure which in her mercy she began.

Father Bonaventure offered the Holy Sacrifice of the Mass on the miraculous altar. Each time he glanced heavenward he failed to see the benevolent image of Mary; it seemed as if a mist or veil covered his eyes. Nevertheless, the unfortunate priest continued in prayer and with a firm faith in Mary did not weaken. The Consecration of the Mass neared and it was here that the consecrated hands of the priest were to elevate the Sacred Species for the adoration of the faithful. It was this movement that influenced the lovable Lady of Czestochowa to perform a miracle. The moment that the hands of the sickly priest elevated the Sacred Host, the rest of the coverings fell from his eyes. At the same time, he saw the Sacramental Species of Christ and above that, set higher on the altar, the picture of Mary. With great inner joy he finished the Sacrifice of the Mass and then told the Paulist Fathers about the miracle.

DROWNING SOLDIER

The following deposition, under oath, was made by Bartlomiej Sanak from the village of Przecisza, county of Wadowicki, located in Little Poland. It was made in person on September 6th, 1855 at Jasna Gora, Czestochowa.

Bartlomiej served in the Austrian Army which, at that time in 1850, was camped in a small village some three miles from Milan, Italy. One evening at about eight o'clock, when darkness had already set in, he was on his way to deliver a message to headquarters. As he groped his way in the dark, he fell into a deep canal, enclosed on both sides by high concrete walls. In vain did he try to get out of the water. The walls were straight and reached high above water level. He swam about for a long time looking for some opening in the wall or some floating object to save his life.

Finally, overcome by fatigue and slowly losing consciousness, he began to submerge in the muddy waters. Before he lost consciousness completely, he suddenly thought of his fatherland — Poland. His beclouded mind concentrated on the one place so dear to the heart of every Pole no matter where one may find himself — the sacred shrine at Jasna Gora, dedicated to Our Lady of Czestochowa.

INSPIRATION

Inspired, he called out loud, "Queen of Heaven and Earth, Madonna of Czestochowa, save me." As if reinforced by some invisible power, Bartlomiej, suddenly felt himself growing stronger. The tired mind became active again so that he could concentrate. He began to swim without difficulty. Swimming up to a pillar, he grasped it and held on for dear life; at the same time, he began calling for help.

RESCUE

Before long, a passerby arrived and dragged him out from the canal without difficulty. As an act of thanksgiving for this miraculous escape from drowning, Bartlomiej Sanak visited Jasna Gora and personally paid his respects to the Madonna.

"MY SON, VISIT ME IN MY HOME AT JASNA GORA"

During the early days of the 17th century, many Polish citizens were enslaved by the marauding Turkish Sultan and his bloodthirsty armies. One of these unfortunate victims was a certain Feliks Skiba. In the year 1617, he was captured, led into slavery and there greatly abused and tortured. After frequently lashing him with a horse-whip, the Turks forced him to extremely hard labor at the point of a bayonet, even though he was underfed and greatly weakened.

FIRMNESS OF FAITH

The chief reason for this abuse was his denial and refusal to bow to the Turkish god and to renounce his Catholic beliefs. Despite all persecution, Feliks became more firm in his faith. What really held him so firm and gave him unshaken courage was his trust and faith in Our Lady of Czestochowa. The firmness and unshaken perseverance greatly pleased Our Blessed Mother.

A VISION

One evening, he retired for the night in his underground dugout, more depressed than ever and under great pain, because his hands and feet were bound tightly with a heavy chain. Suddenly, his cell became resplendent with a supernatural light. This light blinded him and he shielded his eyes against the bright rays. Despite all precautions, the light became more penetrating, and everything around him seemed to be in flames.

Then the air became filled with a strange aroma, sweeter than the perfume of roses and lilies; he heard angelic voices accompanied by the soothing tunes of celestial harps. For a moment, he thought he was in Heaven. In the midst of this resplendent entourage, Feliks saw Our Lady of Czestochowa slowly descend from Heaven and there she stood before him. In front of her, he saw two angels bearing burning torches which reflected her heavenly beauty. Slowly the Blessed Mother approached him, and placing her merciful hands on his head, consoled Feliks in his suffering as she said, "My son, visit me in my home at Jasna Gora."

LIBERATION

As a sign that all this which transpired was not a dream but a reality, the heavy chains were loosened from Feliks' hands and feet at the command of Our Blessed Lady; the doors opened themselves and the prisoner walked to freedom, passing many sleeping Turkish guards and soldiers. For a long time, he wandered through Turkey but somehow the pursuing Turks never recognized him.

Finally, he arrived in his native Poland and answered the invitation of the Blessed Mother when he made a call at the shrine at Jasna Gora. There, in all humility and sincerity of heart, he thanked the Blessed Mother for his liberation.

CONFIDENT WIFE

During the frequent wars of the Hussites in the early 15th century, the heretical hoards broke into Poland in 1432. There was a certain citizen of Raciborz in Slash, who had the great misfortune of being taken into captivity by the invaders and carried away.

The heretics tried their utmost to force him to apostasy since he was a practicing Roman Catholic. They tried peaceful means but when these did not produce the desired results, torture and even scourging were used. In spite of all this, the faithful Catholic stood firm by the faith of his fathers, so he was condemned to death.

EXECUTION

The captors led him beyond the city limits and on the appointed day hung him on some improvised gallows. As he hung there suspended, he commended his soul to the mercy of God and the care of the Blessed Mother.

At that very moment, his pious wife, not even knowing what was transpiring, became greatly disturbed about her husband. He had left home some two years ago and she knew nothing of his present whereabouts. Greatly tortured by an unknown fear about her husband's fate, she turned to Our Blessed Mother for help and consolation. She entrusted her husband to the Madonna's care and promised that if no misfortune befell him, she would make a pilgrimage to Jasna Gora on foot.

The heretics, after performing the execution according to sentence imposed, left the body hanging on the scaffold. They did this so that the spectacle would serve as an example of what would happen to all those who refused to join them in heresy. Before leaving for their homes it was decided to remove the body the following day. The suspended corpse was tossed about by the merciless wind, even the ravens and crows began to fly around to feed on the remains.

RESURRECTION

Towards evening, a soldier rode by and seeing the hanging body, cut the rope with his sword and the heavy corpse fell to the ground. But, lo and behold! The dead man, as if awakened from a deep sleep, rubbed his eyes and was somewhat surprised that he was alive. He walked safely through the encamped heretics, and finally arrived at his home. His devoted wife, overcome with joy, pleaded for an explanation and reason for his extended absence.

EXPLANATION

She was terrified to learn of his experiences relative to the hanging and miraculous resurrection. The account of the events could not be finished until she told her part in it. She explained to her husband about her ceaseless prayer, so full of confidence in the power of Our Lady of Czestochowa, and her promise to the Mother of God. Thus, seeing the miraculous intervention of God in all that transpired, full of gratitude and thanksgiving, they completed the pilgrimage on foot.

BLIND PILGRIM

In 1631, a blind woman from the town of Strykowa came to Jasna Gora. As she was led into the chapel, she knelt by the gates and began to beg Our Lady for a miracle. At that moment, the Benediction of the Blessed Sacrament was taking place. As the woman prayed, the priest carried the Blessed Sacrament by the place where she knelt and at that moment her eyes were opened. At one glance, she saw Jesus Christ exposed in the Monstrance and the portrait of Mary on the altar. Christ heard Mary's plea for a miracle at Cana. Here also, at the request of Mary, the eyes of this maiden were cured miraculously by Christ.

Through the intercession of Mary, the blind see, the deaf hear, the mute speak, the lame and the crippled are cured.

MOCK TRIAL

It was the year 1564. In the peaceful village of Zborow, in the county of Kalis, a group of teen-age youngsters were conducting a mock trial. They appointed judges, the attorneys for both sides, the victims or culprits to be judged and the executioner. The villain was Valentine Zeroniski, the son of the town solicitor. After a childish but lengthy trial, Valentine was found guilty and sentenced to be executed by hanging. The appointed executioner, with the help of the other children, placed a rope around the neck of the condemned playmate and managed to hang him on a limb of a nearby tree. Great was the joy of the witnesses. It seemed to them that Valentine was such a good actor. He gave them such a good performance of the hanging that it looked real as he kicked with his feet. But their pleasure turned to a nightmare as they saw his face grow pale and then a purple blue. Overcome with fear, they tried to take the now lifeless body down from the scaffold; but their boyish strength was not enough to even budge it. Filled with terror, they fled the place of execution and, fearing punishment, told no one of the incident.

Evening came and then darkness as the sun hid behind the distant horizon. The six o'clock Angelus had already rung and the cattle were put away for the night. The children, tired but happy after a long day, were preparing for bed but Valentine did not return. Mrs. Zeroniska, surprised that her son had been gone for some three hours, a thing he had never done before without telling her, called his name, pleading for an answer, but merciless death had paralyzed his vocal cords and held him tight in its bony fingers; he could not answer.

The frightened parents began to search in the neighborhood but to no avail. Finally, late at night, searching in the light of lanterns and burning tapers, they found what was left of their son hanging on the branch of a willow tree. In vain did they try to bring him back to life with artificial means — even with their own breath they tried to warm him up and restore his normal breathing. In vain did the grief-stricken father listen for a heartbeat — their son was dead.

In apparent despair, the parents fell on their knees and offered the dead child to the care of the Madonna of Czestochowa — pleading for mercy. A miracle took place! The Blessed Mother, recalling the moment after crucifixion when she too held the dead corpse of her Divine Son on her knees (how her heart was overflowing with grief and sorrow!), was overcome with compassion for this unfortunate mother. The Queen of Jasna Gora restored the son to life. Valentine opened his eyes wide as he looked about and then, rose up well and alive.

One of the beautiful frescos on the ceiling of the chapel on Jasna Gora, to this day, announces to all visitors the fact of this miracle.

BROKEN BODIES

Jan Wieliczko was a miner and operated a small shaft some sixty feet deep. One day in 1643, he took his son, Wawrzyn, and armed with all the necessary tools of their trade, started his descent into the mine on a single rope.

ACCIDENT

As they were descending, the rope gave way without warning, and both fell to the rocky bottom below. All the mountaineers of the countryside soon assembled at the scene of the catastrophe and, with difficulty, brought the two lifeless bodies to the surface. They were so badly crushed and mangled that no one could so much as hope for their survival. It seemed that they were beyond all human aid.

REACTION

Instead of despair, the assembled people fell on their knees and in suppliant prayer, turned for help to Our Lady of Czestochowa, begging for mercy towards the two unfortunate victims.

The Madonna of Jasna Gora who never refused help to those who turned to her, did not turn a deaf ear to their voices. Suddenly, the two men stood up healthy and well. With all those present, they joined their voices in singing the praises of the Blessed Mother.

THE KING'S SECRETARY

Lambert Urejder was the secretary of King Zygmunt III. Upright, sincere and pious, he was always held in high esteem both by the king and the entire court. Even the people had respect for his qualities and he led a very happy life performing his duties in excellent fashion.

ACCUSATION

It is a fact of actual experience, however, that every human being will sooner or later find in his entourage of friends someone who will betray his confidence. This is exactly what happened to Lambert. Among the supposed friends of Lambert were found those, who moved by jealousy, accused him of receiving secret communications from Tsar Maksimilian. Such communications would naturally lead to the violation of some secrets of the state.

King Zygmunt, misled by the treacherous and sly calumniators, ordered his secretary to be thrown into prison. Lambert remained in prison for some months under the most difficult conditions. His eventual plight, according to the Polish penal code, was to be deprived of citizenship and be deported from the country. His family, until now held in high esteem by all, was greatly humiliated and even hated. As a result, they went into seclusion in near despair. The king, greatly angered by the apparent betrayal of his favored secretary, even refused the family an audience. His former friends and associates left him, and the family, looking upon him as a detestable criminal, refused to have anything to do with him. Everybody awaited the disgraceful trial and its final verdict which was soon to follow.

EXPOSÉ

Abandoned by his people, Lambert betook himself to the Mother of the Most High and Just Judge, the Blessed Mother, residing on Jasna Gora. When all seemed to be lost, he lay prostrate on the cold prison floor, and for hours pleaded with the Blessed Mother to prove his innocence. In return, he promised a special visit to her shrine.

On the third day of continuous confident prayer, the king uncovered, under the most unexpected circumstances, the plot which was planned against Lambert by some unscrupulous and jealous courtiers. The king immediately freed the prisoner and after rewarding him for the unnecessary suffering, reinstated him to even greater favor and responsibility than ever before.

The secretary, grateful for this special grace received from the Blessed Mother, spent five days with his entire family on Jasna Gora in grateful thanksgiving.

IN THE TOWN OF KAZIMIEROW

Maciej and Jadwiga Klimczak, residents of Kazimierow, were blessed by God with a little daughter, Ema. The healthy little girl was a source of great joy and consolation to the devoted parents. In 1598, Ema was two years old.

ACCIDENT

One day, in the absence of the parents, the babysitter, trying to amuse the little tot, sat her down on a stool near an open window. Ema was overjoyed as she sat there, high above the surrounding countryside. Unconsciously, the babysitter, in a moment of forgetfulness, stepped away from the child and as fate would have it, Ema lost her balance and fell out of the opened window to the ground below. The terrified girl ran down to pick her up, but when she arrived little Ema was dead.

As soon as the parents learned of the tragedy, there followed a scene of heartbreaking sorrow. The once happy household was completely disorganized and thrown into chaos. The parents were torn between sorrow on the one hand, because they lost their only child, and anger on the other, over the negligence of the careless babysitter.

It is a known fact, however, that sorrow and suffering can never bring the dead back to life, no more than the lamenting and despair of the unhappy parents.

PREPARATION FOR BURIAL

They soon realized this. They dressed their little Ema in white burial clothes as befits a small, innocent child. On her head was placed a green wreath resembling a crown, and in her pale little hand, they placed a holy card with the image of Our Lady of Czestochowa. Then the vigil began, and instead of the once cheerful laughter of the little child, all that could be heard was the lament and crying of the grief-stricken parents.

With heavy hearts, they stood above the little casket bearing the mortal remains of their earthly treasure. As they stared at dead little Ema, their eyes centered on the image of the Miraculous Madonna of Czestochowa in her hands. Suddenly, as if their numbed minds were illuminated by a miraculous flash of light from above, they both exclaimed simultaneously, "The Lady of Czestochowa, in her goodness, she brought so many other back to life — she will help us — she will not refuse our plea and supplication.'"

THE PILGRIMAGE

Nothing else having been said, they took the opened little casket into their wagon and started towards Czestochowa and Jasna Gora. The journey continued all day and as they traveled along, it seemed that the bright sun tried to refresh the exposed little face of Ema with its bright rays. In vain, during the night, even the bright moon tried to open the once bright eyes now closed forever by the hand of death. The first, second and third days had already become history, but the parents continued their journey. The only disturbance of the tomblike silence was occasionally brought about by their audible prayer.

They were driven on by a deep rooted faith, one which can, as the Gospel states, move mountains. Raised in prayer, their depressed hearts were overflowing with hope and love towards the Blessed Mother. They were guided by a firm faith that the Help of Christians would not disappoint them at this moment of sorrow. They were sure that the Madonna of Jasna Gora was with them.

The fourth day finally arrived. Just about one-half of the journey to Czestochowa had been traversed. The wagon was drawn ahead, never stopping. Likewise, the faith and confidence of the parents grew more firm and intense until finally it reached its climax.

THE MIRACLE

The eyes of Maciej and Jadwiga were almost closed, swollen from tears and sleepless nights, but by a great force of their will, they kept them fixed on the corpse of the beloved child. Their hearts were no longer their own, but enshrined in the Immaculate Heart of Mary.

Suddenly — behold! a miracle. The little girl began to move; her eyes opened and she arose, alive and well. This is the way the Blessed Mother, Queen of Jasna Gora rewarded the firm faith of the Klimczaks.

THANKSGIVING

Overjoyed and happy, they arrived at Czestochowa to officially thank the Blessed Lady of Jasna Gora.

THE ACCUSED

It was in 1609, in the city of Dolsh, in the vicinity of Poznan, that Walenty Uszkowski made a solemn vow to visit Czestochowa, on foot, if spared from the then raging pestilence. He was a pious and devout servant of the Blessed Mother, and in this instance, she heard his prayers. Walenty and his entire household were spared from infection and horrible death. Soon after the passing of the pestilence, he fulfilled his promise and made the pilgrimage to Jasna Gora.

While traveling on foot to pay his respects and offer thanks to Our Madonna, a crime was committed in the vicinity and the culprit escaped. The angry people in pursuit of the perpetrator soon lost track of him but came upon Walenty walking along the roadside where the criminal had allegedly fled. So naturally, in the moment of excitement, a terrible mistake was made and he was accused of the crime. In spite of his protests, resistance and pleas, the angered self-appointed court of justice, inflicted bodily harm on him. Then they cast him into a prison, keeping him there under the most rigid and severe conditions, bound in heavy chains.

So, unjustly accused and shocked by the sudden turn of unexpected events, Walenty fell on his knees and, raising his arms in prayer, turned to his most Holy Protectress for help and deliverance. That very night, the shackles locked around his wrists and ankles fell off and Uszkowski, unseen by the extra guards around his cell, escaped to freedom.

This, however, was not the end of the trials and tribulations permitted by Almighty God to try the faithful servant.

ESCAPE

On the second day of freedom, he was recaptured and placed into the most solitary confinement where he was chained to a heavy iron bar, so that escape would in no way be possible. Walenty, however, did not curse his captors, neither did he try to escape nor to despair, but accepted his new misfortune with resignation and patience. He turned to Our Lady of Czestochowa with great faith and confidence in her power to free him again. Here he made a firm promise and resolution, that when liberated, he would make an offering and change his way of life in order to be more pleasing to God Almighty.

TRIAL

The day of judgement and trial was finally at hand and stern judges took their seats in the courtroom. The innocent looking prisoner was placed before them. Within a short time the court was convinced of his sincerity and innocence after hearing the entire history of events. The turning point of the trial was the recounting of the miraculous escape of the accused and the special assistance given by the Blessed Mother. The verdict of not guilty was given and after excusing themselves, the judges gave Walenty a purse and sent him on his way to Czestochowa with their best wishes.

For the second time Uszkowski, now free and happy, went on his journey to Jasna Gora, where after offering gifts and grateful prayers to our Madonna, he returned to his home to lead a long and God-fearing life with his family.

THE UNFORTUNATE FIRE FIGHTER

A certain night in 1672, the heavens were lit up by an aurora from a burning fire. This took place near the home of Philip Wotucki. At the sight of this tragic incident, Philip called the neighbors to help in fighting the fire. He mounted his horse and, with great speed, headed for the disaster area. Unfortunately, as he sped by, he was struck across the face and eyes by the low-hanging branches of a tree. The pain was so great that he fell from the horse, suffering serious injury. At the outcry of Philip, the neighbors and servants hastily arrived at the scene of the accident, lifted him cautiously and brought him home. His injuries were cared for and the blood washed away, but he sensed that he was blind. The family was deeply saddened.

At a moment's notice the most famous doctors of the area were called, the most expensive and the best medicines were obtained, but all in vain. All were convinced that Mr. Wotucki would remain blind for the rest of his life. During the sad period that followed, Philip was visited by a number of faithful friends. These, in turn, recommended that he should seek relief from his affliction from Our Lady of Jasna Gora. The man was enthused over the encouragement given him and asked some Jesuit Fathers to accompany him to Czestochowa.

THE CURE

They arrived in the evening and immediately sought and found lodgings for the night. Philip's friends retired early but he planned to maintain an all night vigil in prayer and meditation so that he could prepare himself for the ceremonies of the following day at the chapel. His desire was to present himself before the throne of Mary as an humble servant.

During the moments of prayer, his head, covered with many wounds, was pierced by a sudden chill. The change frightened Philip and, as he touched his forehead, blood and matter began to flow from these wounds. He immediately summoned the servant and ordered him to bring a candle. The surprised servant lit the candle and fulfilled the request of the master and gave him a book to read. The master began to remove the bandages which covered his eyes. Lo and behold! — a miracle — he could see again! He began to read from the book without difficulty. In a moment, the Jesuit Fathers approached Philip and they were amazed at this cure. Together they gave thanks to God as they joined in singing the Divine Praises.

That morning, Philip went to the chapel and lying prostrate in the form of a cross, he offered thanks to Mary for the miracle. He lived thirty-nine years after the cure, using the full power of his eyes. It was only a few hours before his death that Mary took away his sight so that he could be received into Heaven.

THE SECRET POWER

Colonel Mikolaj Moczarski was one of the best known personalities during the frequent wars with the Turks from 1590 to 1620. Outstanding for his courage and stout heart, he was always found on the battlefield where the fighting was fiercest. Fear was unknown to him. He was the first man to arrive on the field of honor and always the last to leave.

Many times, we are told, he found himself in extremely difficult situations, where his life was endangered; surrounded by the enemy, but somehow he never lost his nerve and always came out a victor. Bullets fell about him harmlessly, like hail stones, and well aimed thrusts of the lance or sword always missed the mark. Many a gallant horse fell mortally wounded under him but he remained unharmed. It happened quite a number of times that bullets singed his clothes but he himself was untouched. Often friends asked him about the source of his valor and bravery. They wanted to know what protected him from the flying bullets, maybe, they said, he had some mystic power.

To all the inquiries, he would reply — "If you really want to know what keeps me sound and safe, from wounds and death — it is Our Lady of Czestochowa to whom I have been sincerely devoted since early childhood. Behold, this is her shield — a medal suspended from my neck — that is my protection — and another reason is the fact that I never enter a battle without a clean conscience."

This was a confessed secret of a noble soldier, and there were many of these in the Poland of old.

FATHER AND SON

Wawrzyn Prsybetka from Bytomia, blind for a number of years, heard about the miracles at Jasna Gora. The news rekindled a new hope of help from Our Lady of Czestochowa. In 1703, accompanied by his son, he started his journey. Full of zeal they made the pilgrimage to the Holy Place. During the journey, he prayed continuously and as he reached the chapel, he had the feeling of an invisible hand tearing the covering from his eyes. Lawrence was cured miraculously. He saw the people, the altar and, amid the candles, the beautiful picture of Mary and her Divine Son. He was momentarily confused by the course of events; then, suddenly, he shouted forth in appreciation and fell to his knees. From that day on, he was a faithful servant of Our Lady of Czestochowa.

FRIENDS' PRAYERS

One day, in the year 1699, the pilgrims present at Jasna Gora were attracted by the extraordinary appearance of a priest praying before the Miraculous Portrait of the Madonna. They saw him, with tearful eyes, praying with such benevolent ardor that they all surmised that he was making a thanksgiving for some special grace.

The truth was, that Father Albert Mrowczynski, was there at Jasna Gora to fulfill his promise and vow made to the Blessed Mother. This is what he wrote into the records of Jasna Gora.

DEPOSITION

"Nine months ago, I was prostrate with a grave illness. After consulting the different doctors in Sandomierz, Opatow, and Lublin, I used all the medicines prescribed but I did not receive any relief; as a matter of fact, my condition became worse. Time came that I could neither eat nor drink. I felt a terrible burning sensation within me and it seemed that I was being torn apart by some invisible force."

"What aggravated my suffering was the fact, that even during the days of normal health, I was often disturbed by evil spirits especially during Mass, but now the persecutions increased to such proportions that they inflicted bodily harm on me by scourging me to the point of bleeding. At times I saw horrible sights about me; there were beasts, monsters, and serpents — then again, I was brought in view of beautiful and pleasant environments. I saw, during the weird moments, poor helpless souls suffering in terrible fire and I concluded it was either purgatory or hell."

"During these moments of affliction, since I could not speak, I raised my mind and heart to Our Lady of Czestochowa whose sacred image I always carried on my breast."

THE CURE

One time, as I was undergoing the usual affliction of my spirit, I felt I was dying. It was then my friends, the Reformed Fathers, and other acquaintances present at my bedside, offered me to the care of Our Madonna of Czestochowa. After long and fervent suppliant prayers, I arose completely cured, and since then none of these past experiences have ever returned to torture me."

THE NEEDLE

One day, in 1867, a girl named Dorothy Mystkowska, from Kalisz, swallowed a needle while sewing some garments. For three days she suffered terrible pains. She went to several doctors for help, and they prescribed different medications but nothing helped to ease the pain. Instead, it became worse. Her mother, a very pious woman, turned to Our Lady of Czestochowa asking relief from the terrible pains suffered by her daughter. She made a novena with this intention at St. Joseph's Church.

The girl could not eat for several days, suffering terrible discomfort from the injuries caused by the needle. Although suffering great agony from constant pain, she did not stop her prayers to the Blessed Mother of Czestochowa.

It was on Saturday, the second day of the novena, that the sick girl suddenly felt relief from the pain in her abdomen. Touching her right side, she felt something rigid. It was the needle, which she removed with her fingers.

Being miraculously cured, Dorothy and her mother made a pilgrimage to Our Lady of Czestochowa, leaving the needle before the altar as a votum in thanksgiving.

ACCIDENTAL DEATH

There was a watchman at Jasna Gora known as Kazimierz Kozlowski. One day in 1745, while performing his duty near the monastery, he noticed that one of the guests, Jakub Komorowski from Sierodz was rather nasty in his speech and annoyed others. He asked him to refrain because his behavior was the cause of much anger and dissatisfaction. This friendly warning not only did not stop Komorowski but led to more intense insults and made him more audacious. Kozlowski then took matters into his own hands to punish the boisterous villain. He intended to strike him only on the back with his watchman's stick but as fate would have it, the blow landed on the head of Komorowski, and he fell dead.

At the sight of this unexpected turn of events, everyone was greatly frightened, especially the guard himself. Soon he was bound in heavy chains and imprisoned in the adjacent fortress. The court was called to order, and without much deliberation, because they considered the case quite evident, condemned Kozlowski to be shot to death.

Unfortunate, indeed, was the accused killer. It was true that he killed a man but he had no intention of doing so — it was entirely accidental and for that reason he could not understand the rigid sentence imposed. His only intention was to bring an unruly guest to order. Now he was to die the ignominious death of a murderer!

EXECUTION

The chaplain, Father Constantine Pawlowski, arrived to prepare the condemned man for death. After encouraging him to have faith, he gave the victim a small picture of the Madonna of Czestochowa and, bidding him farewell, departed. In a short while, a guard of ten soldiers came into the prison, and with all the usual precautions in handling a murderer, led Kazimierz out to the open field where he was to be shot to death. The usual crowd of curious people accompanied the unfortunate man and his personal entourage.

ACT OF FAITH

On their way to the field, they had to pass by the chapel of St. Rock. Passing by the church, he turned his tearful eyes towards this house of God and began to pray — "Most Merciful Lady, for ten solid years I served faithfully in this your citadel and now I must die ignominiously in such sad circumstances. Please have mercy on me and I will again serve you 'til my last breath as the least of your servants."

MIRACULOUS ESCAPE

Certain people, knowing his noble and pious character, tried to intercede for him, but the judges would not listen and refused to acquit him. Finally, they arrived at the spot prepared for the fulfillment of the imposed sentence and tied Kozlowski to a pillar. The firing squad was called to attention, then ordered to aim and the signal was given to fire. They fired in unison as one rifle. But behold, the intended victim did not slump to the ground as everyone expected, because the ten bullets which were fired struck his chest and fell harmlessly to the ground. Everyone in the huge crowd saw this and confirmed it to be a fact.

Confronted by this miraculous escape of Kozlowski's, they did not know what to do with him in the confusion that followed.

RETURN TO JASNA GORA

Then gathering composure they led Kazimierz back to Jasna Gora where, under oath, a report of the day's happenings was made before Church authorities.

The Primate of Poland, Stanislaus Szembek, Archbishop of Gniezno, happened to be there at the time. He immediately appointed a special commission composed of noble and respected men to investigate the case. Their exhaustive report confirmed the above mentioned facts that Kazimierz Kozlowski, the watchman from Jasna Gora, was known by all for his honest and very religious character. Even those who had to perform the execution because of call of duty, agreed that here we had a real miracle.

The grateful watchman returned to his former service at Jasna Gora to serve more piously and fervently than ever before, grateful for the preservation from certain death.

THE THREE SCARS

One evening in 1430, the sky above Czestochowa and the encircling territory was brightly illuminated by the reflection from the burning countryside. This was but one of the many results of frequent Hussite invasions. After their passing, the grounds were usually literally covered with the emaciated corpses of those who were once loyal citizens of Poland.

Since the monastery at Czestochowa had no standing garrison, many Pauline Fathers gave their lives in the defense of this shrine. The ruthless heretics forced their way into the monastery on this occasion, plundered and robbed it of all its treasures. Among the items stolen was the sacred Portrait of the Madonna which they confiscated along with other spoils.

After throwing the Portrait into a wagon drawn by two horses, they headed southward. However, when they came to the place where the church of St. Barbara now stands, the horses stubbornly refused to go any further. The drivers resorted to all possible means, including the whip, to force the horses to move but to no avail.

DESECRATION

Finally, in order to lessen the weight of the wagon, they threw the picture of Our Lady on the ground. One of the villains, taking his sword, struck the face of Our Lady leaving on it two scars. The picture itself broke into three parts. Not being content with this, the wicked Hussite wanted to strike the picture a third time. Just as he raised his hand to do so, however, a bolt of lightning struck him dead. His colleagues seeing this fled in fear.

PRAYER

When the monks, who were scattered in various directions returned to the monastery, they found the Miraculous Picture missing. They immediately followed the path of the robbers and found the picture smashed, scarred and covered with mud. Greatly moved at this sight, they searched for water in order to wash the picture. Not a drop was to be found anywhere. They fell to their knees, crying bitterly; they asked God's pardon for this unfortunate catastrophe which befell the picture. They expressed their sorrow for not being able to find any water with which to wash the mud off the picture. The Good Lord mercifully answered their supplication. At that very moment, out of nowhere, appeared a spring of crystal clear water. Overjoyed with this miracle, the Pauline Fathers washed the picture and then reverently carried it back to Jasna Gora.

From that day, the spring became a source of great benefits with which Our Lady endowed those using the water. In memory of this miracle a wooden cross was erected and later a chapel was built. Cardinal Maciejowski set aside a certain sum of money for the construction of an ostentatious chapel but his plans did not materialize due to his death. Princess Lubomirska had the place enclosed in a wall and in the XVII century, Father Andrew Goldonowski erected the church of St. Barbara and rebuilt the chapel in which the spring is found. Today there is a well from which pilgrims may obtain the miraculous water.

RELEASE FROM CHAINS

During the reign of King Augustus II, the Polish nation, stagnant in idleness, was the least disturbed over the boundaries of the republic. Neighboring countries, although enemies, ruled the Polish land freely. It was at the command of the Austrian and Prussian kings that Polish citizens were compelled to serve in the respective armies.

Such was the case of Albert Pisarczyk. He was forced to serve in the Austrian army and in turn was sent to fight in the Turkish war, where he was taken prisoner. Albert was sentenced to the dungeons in Belgrade were he was placed in chains, and underwent many torments at the hands of the infidels, who prided themselves in the art of torturing prisoners.

For seven years he endured all the trials patiently, with a feeling, however, that sooner or later their inevitable end must come. With firm faith, he begged Our Lady of Czestochowa for relief from these afflictions and release from prison.His perseverent and sincere prayer to Mary, coupled with a promise of a visit to Jasna Gora touched her heart, for finally he was freed. The shackles on his hands and feet fell off miraculously. These chains he took with him and, passing unseen by the prison guards, he crossed the entire country 'til he reached Czestochowa. It was at Jasna Gora that he offered the prison chains to Mary as testimony of his miraculous release from captivity. This took place in 1705.

UNGRATEFUL JUDGE

I

There is no sound more penetrating and at the same time more depressing than the death toll of a church bell at early dawn. All the townspeople of Nowograd experienced just such a feeling on the morning of 1680, the day that Judge Mikolaj Grocholski was to be buried. He died after a long and painful illness.

FUNERAL ALL ARRANGED

Every member of the bereaved family was there, and all the friends and relatives arrived to pay their last respects to the man whom they all loved so dearly. According to an old Polish custom, the grave was dug and decorated. A special buffet lunch was prepared in the house of the deceased to receive the mourners as guests after the burial service.

At the appointed hour when the pall-bearers raised the casket with the remains of the Honorable Judge to transport it on their shoulders to the waiting hearse, to the surprise of everyone, the judge sat upright in the coffin. At first, terrible confusion ensued as everyone ran away, believing it to be a ghostly apparition. After a while when they saw that the judge was real flesh and blood, really and actually alive, they questioned him how he came back from the dead.

This is what the judge said: "When I was dying and could not confess my sins because I lost my power of speech although still conscious, I raised my heart to God, and begged the Madonna of Czestochowa to restore my health and life, making a promise to visit Jasna Gora. Now I have come back with her help to confess my sins and do penance for them."

These words about the Blessed Mother's power before the throne of God, coming from such a personality who had already crossed the threshold of eternity, produced a profound impression on all present. The lunch prepared for the mourners was changed into a veritable banquet of thanksgiving.

PROCRASTINATION

Despite this great and evident grace and miracle, the judge was rather slow in fulfilling his vow and promise. After a short time, he again became seriously ill. It seemed that this time nothing could save his life. Just when the final moments of his life seemed to be at hand, with a truly contrite heart, Judge Grocholski again turned to the offended Mother of Czestochowa. He expressed his deep sorrow for being so ungrateful, begged for another chance to prove himself and renewed his vow. That night, he received an inspired warning not to procrastinate but to fulfill his promises and vows immediately. The following morning he arose from his bed full of vigor and health. He left immediately to fulfill his vows and pay his respects at the feet of the Madonna of Czestochowa.

II

BELIEVING JUDGE

The above-mentioned Judge Grocholski had a personal friend in the person of John Klokowski, who as a knight, was a shining example of all the patriotic and knightly virtues. Not long after the judge's miraculous restoration to health and conversion to God, the knight was taking part in military maneuvers. During a drive at full speed, his mount stumbled and fell, throwing the rider so hard that he broke his neck and died. The judge was overcome by the news of the sudden and tragic death of this dear friend. After six hours of travel, he arrived at the scene of the tragedy.

JUDGE ARRIVES

Upon hearing of his arrival, the crowd separated permitting him to come to the corpse lying on the ground. Judge Grocholski picked up the cold stiffening body of his friend and raised his eyes to Heaven, in sincere prayer. It seemed to those present that he was actually looking at a supernatural vision, because his eyes were fixed onto one spot as he spoke to his benefactress, the Queen of Czestochowa. Then he fell on his knees and with a shrill voice, one which penetrated into the very marrow of the people's bones, he called, "O Lady of Jasna Gora, just as you have brought me back from the dead to serve you, please restore him to life so that he, too, can wait on you just as I." All those present joined in a chorus with the judge. The suppliant plea and tearful petition penetrated to the heavenly kingdom to the feet of the Blessed Mother.

PRAYER ANSWERED

The Madonna of Czestochowa, could not remain silent and let pass unnoticed this tearful outcry of her trusting and confident children. She performed a miracle. Before the very eyes of the stupefied audience, Sir Kozlowski, the gallant knight, arose, mounted his waiting steed and went off on a very special journey of thanksgiving to the shrine of the Madonna of Jasna Gora.

HOPE REWARDED

The following incident took place in 1753 in the town of Ropczyca. Mary Blayczelska left her home one day in perfect health. All of a sudden, she felt a sharp pain in her left leg and right hand. She swayed a bit and then, as if struck by lightning, fell to the ground. The neighbors who witnessed this, carried her to her home. The doctors diagnosed her malady as incurable paralysis: Mary was to be an invalid for life. Her family was grief-stricken. If the doctors could not help, then who could?

Fortunately not everyone in the house gave up hope. At least one person was found who had great faith in Our Lady of Czestochowa. This person obtained some oil from the chapel at Czestochowa and anointed the paralyzed hand and leg. After this pious gesture, the invalid, filled with the hope of recovery, fell asleep. Lo and behold, in her sleep she had a vision of Our Lady of Czestochowa in the company of Blessed Father Sacandra. Our Lady spoke to her thus: "Mary, I cured you, arise." — Mary awoke and arose completely cured.

KING JAGIELLO

King Wladyslaw Jagiello of Poland, always a great and devout admirer of the Blessed Mother, was the chief sponsor of the cloister on Jasna Gora.

In 1410, he started out with a powerful army, composed of 100,000 well-trained and equipped men, against the invading Teutonic Knights. Extremely sensitive by nature, the pious king spared no effort to avoid this war, but provoking events and circumstances forced him to start the expedition. The bold and bloodthirsty Teutons frequently invaded and plundered the land of the Poles and Lithuanians. Those whom they did not murder, they carried off into slavery.

THE KING'S CAMP

It was on the 15th of July, 1410, that the two armies lined up in battle array within eyesight of one another. Before the battle, the pious king, accompanied by his entire army attended the Holy Sacrifice of the Mass in the open field. Down on his knees, the king tearfully prayed and begged Our Lady of Czestochowa for help and guidance. He was extremely depressed because he could not entertain the thought that so much Christian blood was soon to be spilled on the field of battle.

THE ENEMY CAMP

On the other side of the battlefield, the haughty and proud enemy made fun of the pious king and his army. They constantly reminded the Poles, that they had more spoons in the army kitchen than swords to fight this impending battle.

After Mass, the king intoned the famous Polish hymn to the Blessed Mother, "Boga Rodzica Dziewica," and as the entire army of 100,000 strong took up the beautiful strains of the hymn, the echo resounded for miles across the green fields of Tonanburg. They all sang, because it was a hopeful prayer reinforced by a firm faith in the powerful intercession of the Blessed Mother.

THE BATTLE

At a given signal both forces made contact; the Teutonic knights inspired by a loud outcry of "*God mit uns*" charged forward as the Poles with a barely audible Hail Mary on their lips met the full force of the enemy. Victory hung in the balance for a long time as the battlefield ran crimson with blood, and dead corpses from both sides covered the blood saturated soil. Then, a critical moment arrived, and it seemed that the Knights would be victorious, as the Polish forces began to fall back, due to complete exhaustion of the outnumbered men. But, behold a miracle.

A MIRACLE

St. Stanislaus, Bishop and Martyr, appeared in person above the faltering Polish forces, now on the verge of collapse and inevitable disaster. This was all that was needed. The soldiers, seeing this vision, took it as a sign from their Queen, the Virgin Mary, to reorganize and rally their forces. Above the din and clamor of battle could be heard the inspired outcry of the Polish Army as they repeated the Holy names of Jesus and Mary. With new vigor they struck back at the over-confident Teutons and within a very short time captured 51 Teutonic standards. The disorganized enemy began to flee in disorder, completely routed.

The captured insignias were brought back to Poland in solemn procession and later placed in the Cathedral of the Blessed Mother in Wawel as a sign of thanksgiving and appreciation.

BELIEVING HUSBAND

Anna, the wife of Blaise Kraszko, was afflicted with a malady of her eyes. Despite all efforts and long medication, all was to no avail. In 1748 her eyesight was so impaired that the doctors pronounced her illness as incurable, stating that she would soon become completely blind.

At this time, it so happened that Mary Konuszewicz, a neighbor, was visiting Anna. It is she who related this incident. Anna was complaining to her, how in a short while she would become totally blind. Her husband, a pious man, could bear this torment no longer. Suddenly, he left the house, and in a few moments returned carrying, with great reverence and care, a small bottle. When asked where he went, he said he suddenly remembered a certain neighbor just returned from Czestochowa who had brought back some holy oil. He went and asked if he could have just a bit to place on the eyes of Anna.

First, he prayed very devoutly and then anointed the eyes. At once the misty cloud disappeared from her eyes and she became completely cured. Thanks again to Our Lady of Czestochowa.

THE DOCTORS GAVE UP

In the year 1752, Hedwig Wolska, from Leczyc after a prolonged illness, suffered the continuous breakage of the bone in her palate. Finally, it came to such a point that she could not open her mouth. Her husband and the rest of the family, disturbed at her condition, called upon famous doctors for help, but they, with all their learning and experience, could not help. They pronounced Hedwig incurable and predicted a dreadful death. There were many tears and much sobbing in the household.

By now, everyone was convinced that since the doctors gave up hope, the only thing left was to await merciful death for the poor soul. Yet, amid all these depressing pronouncements,

Hedwig did not accept defeat. She was convinced that above the old worldly science there was a far greater wisdom, namely the heavenly wisdom of Mary, the Mother of God, who chose Jasna Gora as her throne.

Hedwig, strengthened with a new spirit of firm faith, and led by unshaken hope turned her thoughts to Heaven and said — "Oh Blessed Lady of Czestochowa, hearing of your great miracles, which make you famous, to you I turn and beg that if you so desire that I be cured then I in turn will offer you thanksgiving personally in Czestochowa." She no sooner finished thinking in this manner than the cure took place. She summoned her husband and family, but for them it was difficult to understand. "How is it?" they said, "You who were sentenced to death, and a moment before ready to give up your spirit, now you walk in perfect health?" Yet when they learned how she begged Mary for this miracle, their amazement turned into thanksgiving. This home which some moments before was in tears became a haven of joy and happiness. Later Hedwig Wolska and her husband stood on Jasna Gora thanking Mary and fulfilling their promise.

THE EPIDEMIC

The year 1506 will always be noted in the history of Poland, as the year of the great epidemic. Thousands upon thousands of unfortunate people were victims of this merciless reaper.

Many cities and towns were almost completely depopulated while other localities became cemeteries. Some villages were completely deserted by the people while the cattle and fowl were left behind, abandoned and wandering in search of food to the accompaniment of hungry howling dogs. Sickening odors permeated the air from the unburied cadavers lying around, infecting the atmosphere, and spreading disease to the adjoining towns and villages. There was a terrific shortage of doctors, and grave diggers could not be found.

Those who were still in normal health fled to the forests,

looking for shelter and trying to evade contamination. Weakened, underfed and exhausted after being exposed to the elements they dropped like flies along the roads and adjacent fields.

In the city of Wroclaw, a man by the name of Wojciech was one of those caught in a the web of the raging epidemic. Since the doctors had no effective serum, they simply left him to die like thousands of others. So, he prepared for death like a true Christian should and after receiving the last rites of the church entrusted himself to the will of God.

As he lay on his death-bed praying devoutly, he suddenly saw before him a strange old man, with unusually pleasant features, encircled by a long gray beard, and dressed in white (presumably St. Paul, the hermit). Then the old man came close to him and said, "Make a promise that you will make a pilgrimage to the shrine of Our Lady of Czestochowa and Mary will see to it that your life is prolonged." Surprised, because he did not know where Czestochowa was located, Wojciech was touched by the pious decorum of the stranger and made the promise. Tired and greatly weakened by his malady, he fell asleep. This sleep itself turned out to be a miracle. Upon awakening, Wojciech found himself perfectly well and healthy.

Soon after, Wojciech fulfilled his promise and gave testimony at Czestochowa to the veracity of this miracle.

BURNING LAMPS

Wallace Rakobacki, a student at the Krakow Academy, suffered from a glandular disease. Besides this, he broke out with ugly carbuncles over his entire face making his appearance repulsive. He was very much concerned because all efforts at medication were in vain. Being religiously inclined, he decided to seek Mary's aid. He went to Czestochowa in 1727 and there, falling on his knees, prayed ardently to be relieved of his unpleasant misery. While praying, he cast his eyes on the picture of Our Lady. Then he noticed that hanging nearby, were burning oil lamps. Simultaneously, he felt a mysterious force drawing him toward the lamps and, as if in a trance, he dipped his hand into the oil and massaged his face and neck. Lo and behold, at that moment, the carbuncles burst and the glandular swelling disappeared. He was miraculously cured.

Having thanked Our Lady of Czestochowa, he went to the sacristy where, under oath, he related the incident of his miraculous cure.

BROKEN PROMISE

As it often happens to people, Jan Gaworkowski, a citizen of Szklowa, after enjoying perfect health for a long time, became seriously sick in 1774. The illness left him an invalid, deprived of the use of his hands and legs.

Being a man of wide experience who understood human nature, he knew that human aid was helpless in his case, so somewhat depressed in spirit, he lay in bed meditating on the misfortune which had befallen him.

APPARITION

Suddenly, there appeared a strange lady who was unknown to him standing before him. He was stupefied because he saw resplendent rays of light emanating from this lady towards him and he noticed an indescribable charm and majesty about her.

Then he saw her come closer and she said to him, "Jan, why do you lie this way?" Nervously, he answered, "Because I am very sick and I cannot move." Then the lady asked, "Do you want to get well?" "O Lady," he answered, "may I ask for that?"

The Miraculous Madonna continued — "Once going to Wroclaw you went right by Czestochowa and you did not have the courage and conviction to visit the place of my residence. It seemed rather burdensome to you to pay your respects to the Lady of Czestochowa. Now if you want to get well, go there on foot and thus you will undo the wrong caused by your negligence."

THE PROMISE

Overcome by these words, Jan promised to fulfill to the letter the directives and desire of the lady and lo! immediately he felt a great relief from pain. Although he found much difficulty in walking without assistance, a week later he began walking towards Jasna Gora. Slow and difficult was the journey, but it was full of confidence in the power of the Virgin. He had faith that at her feet he would be cured completely from his affliction.

BROKEN PROMISE

After walking about thirty miles, a rider on a wagon came upon him and seeing the weary traveler asked Jan to ride along with him. Feeling very tired, he accepted the invitation. A few minutes after he accepted the ride, Jan felt a terrible shock of pain as fever began to twist his weakened body and he felt the original malady returning. It then dawned upon him, that by accepting the ride in the wagon, he had broken his promise to the Blessed Mother that he would walk on foot to Czestochowa. He immediately got down from the wagon and as he lay in pain on the bare ground he renewed his solemn promise to Our Lady that he would walk the rest of the way to Jasna Gora. He then felt better and continued the pilgrimage until he arrived at Czestochowa. Upon his arrival, he was completely cured.

ACCEPTED ADVICE

In 1636, Hedwig Pichowska, from Casimer nearby Cracow, became very ill. Her pains were so intense that she lost both her speech and hearing. The poor sick soul, just as deaf and dumb as Lazarus, lay on her cot.

One day the family called the priest to come to the sick lady and asked to prepare her for the reception of the Last Sacrament. The saintly priest, seeing the terrible plight of the poor girl, asked her husband why they did not offer her to the care of the Blessed Lady at Jasna Gora. They accepted the suggestion and on the ninth day when the novena ended a miracle took place. Hedwig arose from her bed, fell on her knees and prayed in a loud voice. The family approached her and they were amazed at what they saw. Hedwig heard one and all and explained that Mary's grace brought about her cure. Later, she made a pilgrimage to Jasna Gora.

DYING MOTHER

In 1725, Mary Gebicka, the mother of eight children, became seriously ill. Besides her physical torture she also underwent moral agony, as she saw her eight little children deprived of a mother's loving care. Her heart was pierced with sorrow as she beheld her children pitifully observing their helpless mother. It seemed that medicine was useless. On February 2, the Feast of the Purification, she was overcome by a fever causing her to lapse into a coma.

One of the neighbors who happened to be present at the time, brought some oil from Czestochowa and with a prayer in her heart, applied a bit of the oil to the lips of the dying mother. In the meantime, all those present, including her husband, began to beg for Our Lady's help. A half hour later the dying mother opened her eyes and completely conscious arose from her bed and asked for something to eat as she was extremely hungry. The happy children fell on their knees and gave thanks to Our Lady for the wonderful miracle.

MERCILESS HUSBAND

In Lwow, there lived Regina Stanistanowicz, a woman who was abused unmercifully by her husband. One day in 1627, in a fit of anger, the husband struck his wife across the face with such force that in a moment the woman became blind. The tragedy frightened Regina and she went to many doctors, tried various medications and all to no avail.

With this unbearable affliction she decided to go to Our Lady of Jasna Gora with a petition. After great difficulty, her journey was finished. In the chapel she saw nothing as she fell on her knees. Raising her hands heavenward and with fervent faith, she begged for mercy. The heart of Mary did not reject her petition. In fact, Our Lady cast her merciful eyes on the unfortunate woman and, in turn, a ray pierced the darkened eyes of Regina — at once she was cured.

RESURRECTION

It was during Lent of the year 1628 that Szymon Wruszewski, a citizen of White Russia, became mortally ill. The depressed family spared no time, money, or effort to help the unfortunate victim, but despite all their efforts Szymon died on Holy Thursday morning.

The usually happy Easter morn, commemorating the joyous Resurrection of Christ, was a day of gloom and deep sorrow for this particular family. It was decided to give Szymon a solemn funeral; consequently, the services had to be postponed until after the usual season of festivities. To the usual tears of penance shed by the faithful when meditating over the death of Jesus on Good Friday, the grief-stricken family of Wruszewski added their own outpouring of a suffering heart. Weeping, they said, "Christ Jesus, who rose from the dead after three days, oh, if only our own Szymon would rise from his coffin through the intercession of

Our Lady of Czestochowa, how joyous would be our celebration; with what happiness we could sing the joyous hymns. It seems so contradictory, but faith can accomplish almost anything." They continued to pray — "Mary can do all. The Madonna of Jasna Gora is ready to answer all the suppliant voices especially of those who beg with confidence."

On Holy Saturday the celebrant had already intoned the solemn Alleluja — Christ has risen! Instead of the clapper for the Gloria, the bells rang out. Their resonance only magnified the pangs of suffering in the hearts of the bereaved family, but at the same time, their faith became more firm that the Madonna of Czestochowa would hear their prayer and Szymon would come back to life. Before sunset, as the last rays hid behind the horizon,the corpse of the dead man was touched as it were by a ray of special grace from Mary — a miracle. Szymon rose from his casket and, together with the overjoyed family, sang out hymnal praises to the resurrected Lord and His Mother, famous for her miraculous power on Jasna Gora. In unison they sang a joyous Alleluja whose echo resounded to the gates of Heaven.

As an act of thanksgiving to the Blessed Mother, Szymon Wruszewski personally visited Czestochowa and adored at the earthly throne of the Queen of Jasna Gora.

THE SWALLOWED KEY

One day in 1668, the son of Mr. Peter Rozdzielski, the blacksmith, was playing with a key. He put it in his mouth and while giggling, swallowed it. At first he was sorry that he lost his toy, but when he felt pain in his stomach, he ran to his mother crying, "Mother, the key in my stomach hurts me." The mother was greatly frightened. She asked, "What kind of key, Tommy? Where is it?" "I put it in my mouth and I have it no more. Oh, how it hurts me." He was wailing in terrible pain. Now the poor mother understood what had happened. In her grief she ran to the neighbors for help. Many came proposing different remedies, but nothing brought relief to the sick child. Finally, they summoned a doctor. He tried all sorts of gadgets to remove the key but found he was helpless.

The afflicted mother turned now to Our Lady of Czestochowa and, taking the child in her arms, carried him before the shrine, begging for help and promising at the same time to make a pilgrimage if the child's health would be restored. Praying thus with faith and confidence that her prayer would be heard, she noticed that Tommy had become quiet and stopped crying. The next day the key came out without any pain, and without doing any damage to his body.

Shortly after this happening, the mother and the boy made the promised pilgrimage as a thanksgiving for the miracle.

A DECAYING BODY

In 1752, Mary Teresa Langhammer, from the city of Olbendorff in Upper Silesia, was overcome by a mysterious illness. For some unknown reason her body began to decay. It seemed the doctors could find no cure as she lay in bed for three years suffering from intense pain. So much so, that even her parents couldn't endure it any longer. They prayed that God would take her and relieve her of this misery. On the advice of one of the neighbors they began a novena to Our Lady of Czestochowa, asking that God's will be done — either to take her or to cure her. They promised, that if in God's will she were to recover, they would make a pilgrimage to Czestochowa. Next, they placed their trust in Mary and, having obtained some of the miraculous water, they bathed her decaying body. The result was instantaneous. Mary Teresa felt a great relief and within a week she was completely cured with the exception of a mark on her leg due to a tightening of a nerve. On the 15th of August, Mary Teresa, accompanied by her father, came to Czestochowa to pay a tribute of gratitude to Mary.

THE PILGRIMAGE

It happened in 1749 that a group of pilgrims numbering some one hundred individuals was retuning from Jasna Gora. Their homes were located in Moravia.

RETURN HOME

To reach these homesteads, it was necessary for the weary travelers to cross the Oder river The only means of crossing at that time was a small privately operated ferry boat. The pilgrims boarded the little craft and as it floated across the rapid river, a tragedy interrupted their progress.

ACCIDENT

Due to the inexperience of the crew, the ferry suddenly leaned over to one side, and half of the passengers were thrown into the churning water. Great indeed was the panic both among those remaining on the boat as well as those who watched from the shore. The plight of those thrown into the water was much worse. Many calling for help were sinking, some because they did not know how to swim and others because of shock.

However, this group was not an ordinary one, because each and every one of them without exception, was a particular admirer of the Madonna of Czestochowa. They had just proven their complete faith in her. They spent the last few days visiting her at Jasna Gora where they were blessed with so many graces and consolations.

INVISIBLE AID

As if by some inborn instinct, at this critical moment, all their thoughts and hearts turned to Mary for help. Those on the ferry as well as those on the shore, fell on their knees and as their voices blended together, they pleaded, "Our Lady of Jasna Gora save us." Suddenly, all the people in the water, tossing about, were lifted up by some unseen force and directed to the shore. All were accounted for but four persons and every one believed them to be drowned. When again a miracle! They too were tossed on the shore by the waves, in perfect health.

This miracle was recorded in the annals of Jasna Gora by a certain Jozef Cerka, who was a member of this pilgrimage.

THE COUNTESS

For eight years the Countess Mniszchowna of Lubomir suffered from a painful malady which troubled her very much. Besides this, she was burning with fever and getting worse from day to day.

When neither the doctors nor their prescribed medicines helped her, she decided to go to Czestochowa. She went to Czestochowa in 1744 where she spent several days in prayer and performed works of mercy. Having heard of the miraculous water from St. Barbara's, she too wished to obtain some. As she arrived at the spring, she noticed a great number of pilgrims taking water. Some poured it into bottles, others into larger containers, while others still were drinking it or placing it on their wounds. Seeing this, the countess whispered a prayer to Mary and then drank some of the water.

At that instant, her fever disappeared along with her weakness. She was completely cured. Once again Our Lady triumphed.

BURIED ALIVE

It was a beautiful spring morning in 1748. A babysitter took her little charge, two year old Anna Gorniakowna, for a walk on the outskirts of the town of Lancuc.

The child, stimulated by the refreshing atmosphere of the bright day, was unusually full of life and ran about joyfully, bubbling with energy. Suddenly, she became interested in a cave, dug into the side of a nearby hill.

CAVE IN

Taking advantage of the inattention of the nurse, little Anna hid within the cave. Without warning, there was a landslide and the sandy walls of the cave closed in, completely burying the imprisoned victim. Terrified at the sight, the nurse ran about frantically calling for help. Soon helpful people began to dig madly and for over two hours they worked sparing no effort. Finally, they reached the little girl and found her body bruised, cold, and already changed to a deathly purple hue. Little Anna was dead.

The mother, by now on the verge of collapse, could not convince herself of the reality, that her beloved child was dead. She could not understand how so short a time of two hours, could rub out the life of this child for all eternity.

Despite everything, her faith in the Blessed Mother was not shaken. she took the limp little body in her arms and with her heart raised to Mary in fervent prayer, she carried the remains of Anna into the Church of the Dominican Fathers. In vain did her friends and relatives try to stop her. She did not even hear their protesting voices as they called after her, "What are you doing? The girl is already dead. At least place her in some kind of a casket." All the terrified mother could answer was, "Let me go because I am sure that Mary of Jasna Gora will restore her to me, alive."

She ran into the church, and with a fervent prayer placed the child in the care of Our Blessed Mother. It was then that she made a solemn promise to visit Jasna Gora as an act of veneration and thanksgiving as soon as her dead daughter was restored to life.

The firm and lively faith of the mother produced a resounding echo from Heaven. Soon, the child opened her eyes and smiled, full of life. Immediately, with a heart overflowing with joy, the grateful mother went to Jasna Gora and offered thanks to the Great Madonna.

DOCTORS COULD NOT HELP

An orphan girl named Marianna Staniszewska, at the age of 17, had to work in a woolen factory in Zyradowie. One day while combing her hair, she put a long, thin pin with a glass head into her mouth. While talking to other girls, she swallowed the pin. Frightened by the accident, she went to the doctor but he could do nothing to remove the pin. For five long years she suffered terrible stomach pains, going from one doctor to another, each comforting her that in time the pains would cease. She lived in hope that it would be so.

In 1865, when she was twenty-two years old, the pains troubled her so much that she almost died. Again she went to the doctors, underwent very scrupulous examinations and to her dismay, found out that she was incurably sick. Knowing that her days were numbered, she offered her soul to Our Lady of Czestochowa in whom she wholeheartedly confided.

She undertook a pilgrimage to the shrine of Czestochowa May 18, 1865. Entering the chapel, she fell on her knees and with tearful eyes begged the Blessed Mother for a cure, presenting at the same time her unfortunate state of life, her pains and all her misery. People who were there saw how miserable she looked, how pale she was, and they all sympathized with her.

While praying so fervently before the Blessed Mother's shrine, Marianna started to cough violently, so much so, that the pin came to her throat and finally dropped out of her mouth onto the floor. The pin which the doctors could not remove and which had given her pain for so many years, now at the command of the Blessed Mother, came out without any earthly help and without a doctor.

Marianna lay prostrate before Our Lady of Czestochowa in gratitude for the miraculous cure, thanking the Blessed Mother with a promise that to the end of her life, she would take the Blessed Mother for her mother and remain a faithful child to her deliverer.

Many people were present when this miracle occurred. In the chronicles of the convent, the following witnesses have assigned their signatures: Reverend Barnabas Ptakowski, Sub-sacristan John Oczko and Joseph Grzybowski.

A CONVERT

Wit Kanka, a Silesian who worked for a Lutheran, had great devotion to Our Lady of Czestochowa. He often visited Jasna Gora and always brought back with him some of the miraculous water from St. Barbara's.

In 1627, a plague struck all the cattle in the village where he lived as well as those in the neighboring towns. The inhabitants were at a great loss. Kanka, seeing this, placed his trust in Mary and sprinkled the cattle with water from Czestochowa. His cattle remained unharmed. The following year the plague returned. Kanka asked his master for permission to go to Czestochowa in order to get a supply of the miraculous water. Having explained the story to his master, Kanka not only received permission but was told to bring him some of the water. Within a short while he returned and the master, even though a Lutheran, placed his trust in Mary and sprinkled his cattle with the water. He did not lose a single one. Impressed by this miracle, he became a Catholic.

BLESSED MOTHER LEADS SOULS OUT OF PURGATORY

This happened at the beginning of the XVI century, in Slavonia. A certain man named Oswald, became seriously ill. Anticipating death and abandoned by the doctors, he turned for help to Our Lady of Czestochowa. He made a solemn promise that in the event that he would be cured, he would make a pilgrimage to Jasna Gora. It seems that the Blessed Mother was delighted with the faith and hope which Mr. Oswald had in her intercession. He was cured miraculously. After his recovery, he somehow delayed fulfilling his promise. A few years passed. Now it happened that Oswald again became serious ill and having received the Last Sacraments, died, without fulfilling his vow. He had a son, who was in school preparing for the priesthood.

APPARITION

Shortly after the death of his father, the young seminarian was sitting in his room preparing his studies for the next day. Suddenly he was startled. He knew that in his room there was no one besides himself, that the door was barred and no one could enter unnoticed, still there was someone beside him. The nebulous figure standing was ghastly shrouded. The boy rubbed his eyes to verify that he was not dreaming, but the figure did not move. It started to come towards him as if flying in the air. Frightened by this apparition, the boy blessed himself, but the spectre did not move nor disappear. It came so close to the boy, that he recognized it to be his dead father. No longer was he afraid, but stretching his hands toward the spectre, called, "Father." The ghost smiled at him with a fatherly gesture, but seemed very sad. He then spoke in a grave tone, that he was under the special protection of the Blessed Mother, but he was suffering in Purgatory for not fulfilling the vow made to her in his recent sickness. God permitted the father to appear to his son, to ask for prayers. Also, when he became a priest, he should make a pilgrimage to Jasna Gora and there offer his first Mass for his father's soul. The good son promised to do this favor for his father. Looking at the boy, the spectre slowly disappeared.

ORDINATION AND FIRST MASS

Several years passed. The son was ordained in 1521. Now was the time to fulfill the promise made to his father and therefore, he prepared to leave for Poland to say his first Mass. His relatives, on hearing of the apparition and the promise made to the dead man, tried to persuade him that it was foolish to believe in apparitions, especially for such a learned man. They tried to convince him that he ought to say his first Mass in his native town and it would be with the same benefit to the soul of his father. Finally, the young priest consented.

On the appointed day for his first Mass, the town of Prywidz was crowded with the relatives and friends of the newly ordained priest. The altar was beautifully decorated with flowers and numerous candles. The tinkling of the bell from the sacristy was heard, announcing that the Mass was soon to start. All eyes were turned toward the altar where the pastor in cope and the newly ordained priest were standing. But, lo! The priest found himself speechless while trying to say the "Introibo." In his distress, he looked for help to the pastor who could not understand what he wanted. By means of signs, he showed that he could not say a word. The frightened pastor turned to the congregation, announcing that, because of the sudden illness of the priest, there would be no Mass said by the newly ordained. The congregation, shocked by the news, left the church. When relatives went to the sacristy to find out what had happened, the young priest wrote: In this event, I presume it is the penalty of God for not fulfilling the promise I gave to my father. The relatives agreed to this, and helped the priest on his journey to Poland.

THE MIRACLE

The mute priest arrived on Jasna Gora, gave an account of his trip, and begged the monks to pray for him. Dressed in liturgical vestments, he approached the altar. He knelt before the shrine of Our Lady of Czestochowa imploring the restoration of his speech and to have pity upon the soul of his dead father. With fear he approached the steps of the altar to begin the Holy Sacrifice. While making the sign of the cross, he suddenly regained his voice. He knew it was through the intercession of Our Lady of Czestochowa. With great emotion he said his first Mass, offering it for the soul of his father.

The following night the ghost of his father appeared to him in glory, thanked him for the favor rendered and reported that he was already in Heaven at the feet of the Queen of Angels.

ATTEMPTED SUICIDE

Andrew Miaskowski, from Poturzyca, was suffering from hypochondria for several years. Finally, in his desperation, he took a dagger and thrust it into his chest. His wife grasped the weapon from him, but when the doctor came and examined the wound, he found the man beyond help and saw that his end was near. The unfortunate man, who now saw what a grievous crime he had committed, became remorseful for this attempt. He pleaded with God to forgive him and after receiving the Last Sacraments, passed away.

ODD NOISES

Deathly silence hushed the village after the death of Andrew. His widowed wife devoted her life to acts of charity and prayer for her deceased husband. One day after the funeral, one of the servants was passing by Andrew's room at noon time. He heard terrible moaning coming from within as if someone was pleading for help. He opened the door, entered, but saw no one in the room. He looked everywhere to find whence the moaning came. Surprised as he was, he went to notify the lady of what he heard, but she did not attach any meaning to the news, since it was daytime and she thought the servant had overheard some noise.

One evening, the moaning was heard again and the voice pleading for help. Terror possessed the whole household, and as the moaning and pleas were repeated at noon and in the evening, all presumed that the room was haunted by some spirit. Now they clearly heard the voice which said, "I vowed that I would fast on Saturdays and make a pilgrimage to Czestochowa, but did not keep my promise. Please, do it for me."

The servant now understood that there must be a dead person doing penance. Terrified, he ran to notify the tenants. Panic reigned in the house. No one dared to go near the room during noon and evening hours, but the moans, pleadings and begging did not cease. Finally, one of the ladies, braver than the others, entered the room, and asked: "Who are you, and what do you want?" She received an answer that the man, proprietor of the house, who died several months ago, was suffering terribly in Purgatory and was pleading for mercy for his soul. He added that he would disturb them until they rendered him the service he asked for. Then the spirit said: "Do charity, give alms to the poor in Czestochowa, have Masses offered for my soul, and then and only then shall I be delivered from Purgatory. On hearing this, the wife immediately fulfilled his request. Soon she heard the same voice thanking her for the favor done for him, helping him to his happiness.

THE MASTER RETURNED

In 1670, Martin Stokowski died leaving a vast amount of earthly riches. His only heirs were his brother, James, and his wife. Shortly after the death of the former lord, one of the servants of the present owners of the estate, saw some sort of figure rising from the ground, entirely surrounded by flames. She became frightened but wanted to be sure that it wasn't her imagination; hence, she peered carefully at the sight before her. Lo and behold! she recognized the figure to be the dead owner of the vast estate, the late Martin. He turned to her and spoke in a sorrowful tone: "Please ask my relatives to come to my aid. I am enduring the most horrible tortures, but I cannot help myself. Ask them to have five Masses said before the portrait of Our Lady of Czestochowa, and then they will come to my rescue." After finishing these few statements, the figure vanished from sight. The servant was terribly frightened and quickly ran to her master and told of all that she saw. It was incredible and James Stokowski did not know whether to believe her or just let the matter pass. Yet, he had no peace. At times it seemed that the girl was day dreaming, but then he began to fear lest his brother might really need his help. Everyone in the house seemed to be depressed because of the incident described by the servant.

THE VISION RETURNS

On the following day, the family of Stokowski, his two daughters and a few servants were gathered in the living room, discussing the episode of the day before, when all at once, all present heard very clearly the voice of the deceased owner. It seemed that the voice was coming from underground. All stood rigid from fright. The sound was repeated a few times, but no one dared to move. After a while an invisible hand began to write with a red-hot coal on the table top. The words could not be understood. Time elapsed before those present could speak and decide what to do. Unanimously, they proposed to fulfill the wish of the deceased and leave for Czestochowa without delay.

Early next morning, the entire family departed for the shrine of Our Lady. At nightfall they stopped at a hotel in Widaw. They seated themselves in the lobby along with the hotel keeper and three merchants from Silesia.

One of the young ladies put her rosary on the table. As they were speaking of their journey to Czestochowa, the deceased

Stokowski stood in their midst. His face was pale and drawn and his body seemed to be coming up from an ocean of fire. Those present froze from fear, dared not move or even breathe. The dead man went to the table, picked up the rosary and held it high in his hands. Suddenly, he dropped it and pleaded that they pray for him. His disappearance was as sudden as his appearance. Those present were dumfounded. After a while, when fear left them, they immediately recited the rosary for his soul.

JASNA GORA

Upon their arrival at Jasna Gora, they had five Masses said for the deceased member of their household. They stayed on and joined in prayers with the priest in the next fifteen Masses, which they offered for the repose of the soul. For the next seven days of their stay in Czestochowa, they prayed fervently and gave alms generously.

On the eighth day, they prepared for their homeward journey. At nightfall they tarried at a hotel and once again the deceased Mr. Martin made his appearance. He began tracing various letters and signs and then a cross — under which he wrote: "Oh if today I could..." and he disappeared. Those present understood that what he wanted to write was his hope of entering Heaven.

That same day at the estate, the same servant who saw him the very first time claimed that, while alone, she saw Mr. Martin passing on to eternal happiness. She saw him as a young gentleman, dressed in a garb as bright as the sun and girdled with purple. He held a candle in his hand. She took an oath that what she said actually happened.

When His Excellency, the Bishop of Cracow heard of this incident, he ordered that it be minutely examined. After the required examinations, he had the case submitted to the archives at Jasna Gora as one of the greatest miracles of Our Lady of Czestochowa.

THE CURE

In 1620, Poland was overrun by a pestilential disease and there was not a home without a corpse. Thousands had already perished and thousands more were struggling for life. Among these was a 20-year old girl by the name of Helen Zajackiewicz who lived in Czestochowa. As the girl lay in her bed, she suffered immensely since her body was covered with painful carbuncles. She was nearing the end when suddenly her mother thought of the water in the miraculous spring at the shrine. Hurrying back from the spring, she sprinkled the girl with the miraculous water while praying to Our Lady. At that moment the carbuncles burst, the scars disappeared and Helen was completely cured, thanks to Our Lady. Many other people were also cured either by drinking the water or applying it to their bodies.

THE BLIND ARTIST

The court artist of King Jagiello, James Wezyk, was afflicted with eye trouble, which resulted in total blindness. The news was received by many with profound sorrow especially by the artist himself who was deeply devoted to his work. Despair overtook him because he realized that never again would he be able to paint, with vivid color, the things of beauty that his eyes presented to him. The help of the court physicians was in vain. The poor artist, living in Wilno, awaited with resignation and intense longing the day of his eternal rest, not for one moment expecting to see the light of day again but only the darkness of his misfortune.

INSPIRATION

In 1392 James found out about Jasna Gora of Czestochowa where a famous painting of Mary, painted by St. Luke as tradition tells us, was honored. He was led to understand that to this portrait of Mary were attached certain extraordinary powers from which many people had already benefited. With this knowledge, the artist, unmindful of the distance between home and Czestochowa and filled with enthusiasm, decided to make the pilgrimage to Our Lady of Czestochowa and beg for the restoration of his sight.

A thousand kilometers separated Wilno from Czestochowa. Nevertheless, with a firm faith, a song and a prayer on his lips, he started his journey afoot. With the help of charitable people he slowly crossed the numerous boundaries and villages, the plains and dark forests, the rivers and the streams.

Finally, after a long lapse of time and many hardships, he stood at the foot of Jasna Gora. He entered the miraculous chapel and falling on his knees began to pray in earnest for the restoration of his sight. At once, his eyes, darkened for many years, were filled with tears and, inspired by faith, he lifted his head slowly toward the face of Mary and begged for mercy. At that moment, an internal voice commanded him to glance in a certain direction where he presumed the picture to be; he raised his face heavenward and began to shout with joy. For the first time he saw the holy picture of Our Lady of Czestochowa, so beautiful, so radiant, so life-like, not as a portrait but as a true and living Madonna. His eyesight was restored and from that day on he consecrated his life to the painting of pictures of Our Lady, his benefactress.

This miracle was verified and confirmed by Bishop Martin Szyszkowski, an eyewitness.

STORY OVERHEARD

In the year 1595, Margaret Pierzchala of Myslenic could no longer undergo the tortures of blindness which had afflicted her since the age of twelve. A cure seemed impossible. On the verge of despondency, she fell into serious temptation by the devil. Disconsolate, she decided to commit suicide. However, after some reflection, she recognized her mistake, when, by chance, she overheard someone speaking of a wonderful miracle which had taken place at Czestochowa. The words affected her deeply and at once she was penitent for her evil intention. She then decided to go to the Blessed Mother in search of a cure for her sickness.

Afoot, Margaret began her journey with a companion. During the trip she renewed her act of faith and trust in the power of Mary. At last she reached Jasna Gora and momentarily became alarmed by the very thought that the Blessed Mother would listen to the petition of a sinner like her. She then remembered that Our Lady is the Refuge of Sinners and the Mother of Mercy; this thought filled her eyes with tears and moved her to sorrow for her sins. In this state of mind, she entered the chapel.

The assembled people watched the young girl as she made her way down the aisle towards the altar. She asked the faithful around her to pray so that together they could implore Our Lady for mercy. Margaret fell on her knees and, striking her breast, begged Our Lady of Czestochowa for a miracle. She then fell prostrate on the floor, hoping and begging unrelentlessly for that miracle. After a moment of prayer, the girl lifted her head. At this time, Our Lady was moved by the tears which expressed firm faith and true contrition; then, the rays from Mary struck the blind eyes. A cure took place. At once the girl saw the beautiful picture of Mary and with a cry of, "I can see," she ran to the altar. Joy filled the chapel and the faithful glorified Mary for her kindness.

THE BLEEDING MAN

This happened in 1784, on an estate in Krzewiny. The administrator of this estate, Francis Bialkowski, while patrolling the forest, noticed a peasant stealing wood. Coming close to the thief, he wanted to capture him and surrender him to the authorities, but the thief seeing that he could not escape, threw himself at the administrator, wounding his face with an axe.

Bialkowski, trying to escape from the attacker, ran to the tree where his horse was tied, but before he could reach the spot, the attacker ran ahead and took the horse by the reins so that Bialkowski stood helpless. Unfortunate Bialkowski, with his blood-smeared face, knew not what to do. Taking advantage of the situation, the peasant again attacked the administrator and knocked him to the ground. Believing that he would be killed, the victim began to pray: "Our Lady of Czestochowa, help me." In the meantime, the angry attacker began to trample Bialkowski; he stabbed him with a rod, and believing that his victim was lifeless, he fled, leaving the bleeding man on the ground.

Many hours passed, the wind murmured among the leaves, the birds chirped their beautiful melodies, the deer came out of the woods, but seeing a man on the ground, made their retreat from whence they came. The wounded administrator woke from his trance; recalling what had happened to him, he understood now that he escaped death although seriously wounded. He cried to the Blessed Mother, "O Mother of God, I thank thee for saving my life." He was able to return home where he recuperated from the wounds.

In gratitude for saving his life and for his recovery, he went on foot to the shrine of Our Lady of Czestochowa where he offered prayers in thanksgiving.

A HOPELESS CASE

During one severe winter, Raphael Zelazowski, from Kovno in Lithuania, froze his hands and feet so that he had no control over them. Then he suffered such terrible pain, that he could not sleep at all; he would wail and moan day and night. There was no relief for the victim and no peace for the family watching him in agony. All possible means were used to alleviate the pain but to no avail; he did not enjoy a moment of relief.

In the summer of 1614, a group of people were making their annual pilgrimage to Jasna Gora. Solicitous neighbors approached the sick man and influenced him to make the trip to Czestochowa. They tried to comfort him to the best of their ability. He wondered how he could undertake such a long journey. He had to be carried from one bed to another; he could not lift his arms nor move his hands. He was an invalid, so why even speak of such a trip? These circumstances depressed him greatly and his life was more miserable.

Nevertheless, the neighbors, expressing pity for the poor man, talked over the situation and resolved to take him along. They lifted Raphael off his bed, dressed him carefully, placed him in a cart in as comfortable a manner as was possible, and offered him to the care of Mary of Czestochowa. The journey covered one hundred miles. The poor man suffered terribly during the entire trip, especially during the night. Often the constant pain and discomfort caused him to emit blood-curdling screams. Yet not for a moment did he lose hope in Our Lady of Czestochowa; continuously and piously, he surrendered himself to the mercy of Mary.

After many days of the tiresome journey, they reached a point were they could see the steeple of Jasna Gora. Joy was expressed by the pilgrims as they all knelt at the sight of the chapel in the distance. The poor unfortunate man began to cry bitterly because he was not able to follow the example of his comrades when, suddenly, he experienced an odd feeling coming over him. He felt neither his feet nor his arms which were usually in pain and extremely heavy. Now they became light and normal, just as before his sickness. He understood at this moment, that at the sight of the steeple of the shrine, he was the recipient of a miracle. In gratitude and love, he shouted joyfully. This stunned the pilgrims because they thought that Raphael was in such pain that maybe the end was at hand. Then he continued to sob, and not being able to talk, pointed to his legs and arms and then to Jasna Gora. They understood that Mary sent aid to this poor man. As the pilgrims approached the hill, the sick man stepped from the cart and walked unaided. As he came through the threshold of the famous chapel, he saw the benevolent look of the Mother of God; he noticed the lovable eyes of Mary looking upon him and relieving the last vestige of sickness and pain.

After making a thanksgiving to Our Lady of Czestochowa, he returned with the pilgrims, walking the entire return trip.

UNCHARITABLE FRIENDS

After a long and troublesome malady of the eyes, Mathew Stanulewicz, a servant from Przemysl, became totally blind. The plight of this poor person was woeful, since no one could help relieve his suffering. He worked hard, as best he could under the handicap, but uncharitable friends caused him a great deal of grief. Under these conditions Mathew soon became disheartened, but as miserable as things were, he continued to pray. Yet, it seemed that the prayers were not fervent enough, because the merciful God did not answer his pleading prayers.

One cold morning, the overlord sent Mathew on horseback to another farm. In his condition he rode carefully, having great faith in the horse. Unfortunately the horse became frightened, threw the afflicted rider from the saddle and ran off. Mathew was greatly disturbed by this incident and began to despair. Without thinking, he made these remarks to God: "Lord, You never wish to be merciful to me. Let the devils come and take me; I do not wish to suffer anymore!" But the all merciful God forgave this unwarranted remark and did not permit the devils to answer this call.

Soon after these blasphemous words were spoken, some strangers came by and took the unfortunate man with them. The first night after the dreadful episode, Mathew had a realistic dream in which he visualized the chapel of Czestochowa filled with people, some of whom were lying in the form of a cross, some were praying and others singing. He was awakened, amazed by this dream but he did not know what it meant. This same scene was repeated five different times. Impressed by the reappearance of this dream, Mathew pondered more seriously and was convinced that this was a sign from Heaven and that he should turn to Our Lady of Czestochowa for help.

Without delay the poor soul began a novena to Our Lady of Czestochowa; he offered himself under her protection and promised to make a pilgrimage to Czestochowa as soon as possible. Mary witnessed this firm act of faith and hope in her and sent him relief because at the conclusion of the novena, Mathew miraculously received his eyesight. After this episode, he came to Jasna Gora on May 17, 1785, fulfilling his promise.

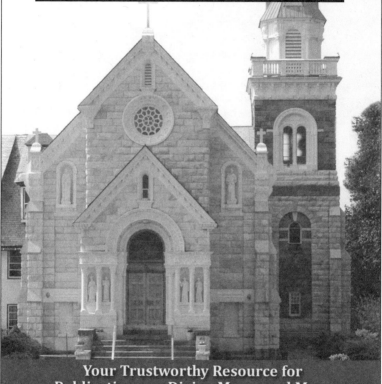

MARIAN PRESS
STOCKBRIDGE · MA 01263

PROMOTING DIVINE MERCY SINCE 1941

Marian Press, the publishing apostolate of the Marian Fathers of the Immaculate Conception of the B.V.M., has published and distributed millions of religious books, magazines, and pamphlets that teach, encourage, and edify Catholics around the world. Our publications promote and support the ministry and spirituality of the Marians worldwide. Loyal to the Holy Father and to the teachings of the Catholic Church, the Marians fulfill their special mission by:

- Fostering devotion to Mary, the Immaculate Conception.

- Promoting The Divine Mercy message and devotion.

- Offering assistance to the dying and the deceased, especially the victims of war and disease.

- Promoting Christian knowledge, administering parishes, shrines, and conducting missions.

Based in Stockbridge, Mass., Marian Press is known as the publisher of the *Diary of Saint Maria Faustina Kowalska*, and the Marians are the leading authorities on The Divine Mercy message and devotion.

Stockbridge is also the home of the National Shrine of The Divine Mercy, the Association of Marian Helpers, and a destination for thousands of pilgrims each year.

Globally, the Marians' ministries also include missions in developing countries where the spiritual and material needs are enormous.

To learn more about the Marians, their spirituality, publications, or ministries, visit **marian.org** or **thedivinemercy.org**, the Marians' website that is devoted exclusively to Divine Mercy.

Below is a view of the National Shrine of The Divine Mercy and its Residence in Stockbridge, Mass. The Shrine, which was built in the 1950s, was declared a National Shrine by the National Conference of Catholic Bishops on March 20, 1996.

© MARIE ROMAGNANO

For our complete line of books, DVDs, CDs, and other trustworthy resources on Divine Mercy and Mary, visit thedivinemercy.org or call 1-800-462-7426 to have our latest catalog sent to you.

BOOKS ON MARY

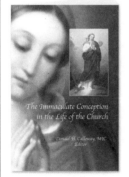

POAL 9781596141957

PUREST OF ALL LILIES: THE VIRGIN MARY IN THE SPIRITUALITY OF ST. FAUSTINA

This was the first book written completely by Fr. Donald Calloway, MIC. "It's basically my licentiate thesis on St. Faustina and the Virgin Mary," he explains. "It was edited to keep it from being too technical for a general audience." The book explores St. Faustina's rich relationship with the Mother of God, as recorded in the saint's *Diary*. Father Donald discusses the important lessons the Blessed Mother taught St. Faustina about suffering, purity of heart, and humility. He also includes an analysis of St. Faustina's poems that often use flower metaphors for Mary. Paperback. 128 pages.

THE IMMACULATE CONCEPTION IN THE LIFE OF THE CHURCH

In 2004, Fr. Calloway edited his first book, *The Immaculate Conception in the Life of the Church.* This collection of essays came from a symposium on the Immaculate Conception for the 150th anniversary of the proclamation of the dogma. Paperback. 198 pages.

ICLC 9781932773934

THE VIRGIN MARY AND THEOLOGY OF THE BODY

In these brilliant essays, prominent experts explore how Pope John Paul II's groundbreaking *Theology of the Body* applies to the Blessed Virgin Mary. Edited by Donald H. Calloway, MIC. Paperback. 285 pages.

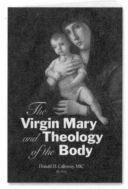

TVM 9781596141360

BOOKS ON MARY

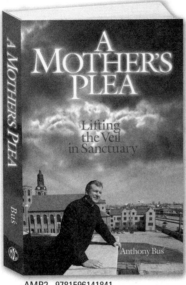

AMP2 9781596141841

A MOTHER'S PLEA LIFTING THE VEIL IN SANCTUARY
Fr. Anthony Bus

In the lonely walk through spiritual dryness when God seems so distant, a woman's voice is heard in the deep recesses of the soul of a struggling priest in a diverse parish. She prods him to discover God and the meaning and purpose of life in the sacred silence of sanctuary. From that space in sanctuary, the veil is lifted and *A Mother's Plea* to her children to seek refuge in God's love and mercy is heard.

Fr. Anthony Bus recounts his journey to fulfill Our Lady's request to make Jesus known, loved, and served. This revised edition brings a long-awaited dramatic finale to the story that promises hope to a suffering world.

A must-read for those on their own path to an authentic spiritual awakening!

392 pages with 19 beautiful full-color images

This is the vividly personal story of a priest in a Chicago parish coming to terms with what the priesthood demands of a man in a great modern city. Profoundly conscious of the sin and unbelief that distort human lives and that touch him too, Father Bus is sometimes desperate in face of the hostile disregard for the Church so prevalent today.

— FRANCIS CARDINAL GEORGE, OMI
Archbishop of Chicago

ESSENTIAL DIVINE MERCY RESOURCES

NEW

AUDIO DIARY OF ST. FAUSTINA

You'll feel like you are actually listening to St. Faustina speak in a gentle Polish accent as she writes in her Diary. Hear this dramatic portrayal of the voices of Jesus and Our Lady. Gain deeper insight into Faustina's mission to share the message of Divine Mercy with the world. **ADCD 9781596142299**

DIARY OF SAINT MARIA FAUSTINA KOWALSKA: DIVINE MERCY IN MY SOUL, DELUXE LEATHER-BOUND EDITION

Share the gift of mercy with this deluxe edition of the book that has sparked The Divine Mercy movement among Christians. Pages come with gilded edges and a ribbon marker. 7 1⁄8" x 4 3⁄8", 772 pages, 37 photos.

BURGUNDY: DDBURG **9781596141896**
NAVY BLUE: DDBLUE **9781596141902**

Hardcover, Trade Paper, and Compact Editions available in English and Spanish.

THE DIVINE MERCY MESSAGE AND DEVOTION

Fr. Seraphim Michalenko, MIC with Vinny Flynn and Robert A. Stackpole.

Outlining The Divine Mercy message and devotion in an easy-to-follow format, this booklet provides an overview to one of the Catholic Church's fastest growing movements. Includes all elements and essential prayers of The Divine Mercy message and devotion.

M17 9780944203583

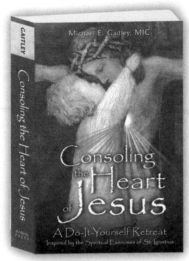